The Diary of the Other Health Freak

Ann McPherson and Aidan Macfarlane

Illustrated by John Astrop

Oxford   Melbourne   Toronto

OXFORD UNIVERSITY PRESS

1996

Oxford University Press, Walton Street, Oxford OX2 6DP

Oxford New York
Athens Auckland Bangkok Bogota Bombay
Buenos Aires Calcutta Cape Town Dares Salaam Delhi
Florence Hong Kong Istanbul Karachi
Kuala Lumpur Madras Madrid Melbourne
Mexico City Nairobi Paris Singapore
Taipei Tokyo Toronto

and associated companies in
Berlin Ibadan

Oxford is a trade mark of Oxford University Press

First edition, under the title I'm a Health Freak Too!, first published 1989
as an Oxford University Press paperback
Second edition, under the title The Diary of the Other Health Freak
first published as an Oxford University Press paperback 1996

British Library Cataloguing in Publication Data
Data available

Library of Congress Cataloging in Publication Data
Data available
ISBN 0–19–286183–2

10 9 8 7 6 5 4 3 2

Printed in Great Britain by
Mackays of Chatham PLC

Acknowledgements

For this new edition we would particularly like to acknowledge the help of Kate Roberts, Alice Coulter, Alice Maclennan, and Laura Harris. We would like to thank them and the many teachers and pupils who kindly commented on and helped update the language and the content of the original book.

Susie's diary is a combination of a large number of different voices and sources. We advertised in *Just Seventeen* and were overwhelmed by the avalanche of pale pink and yellow envelopes that snowed through the letter-box full of wonderful, and sometimes libellous, material.

Three local upper schools in Oxfordshire—Peers, Lord Williams, and Cheney—once again put up with us invading the privacy of their pupils' lives with a detailed questionnaire on AIDS. Some of our children were more enthusiastic than others at contributing this time—Beth, Tamara and Tess, along with Gus, greatly helped in writing parts of it and casting more than a critical eye on the manuscript. Sam and Magnus were notable for their consistent reluctance to reveal any part of their teenage existence, while enjoying the fruits of the first book. For this we can only respect them. Among their many friends who helped us we would particularly like to acknowledge Amanda, Louise, Kitty, Gina and Matthew.

Marny Leech advised us throughout and edited the final manuscript. Jill Challner very kindly gave us the tables we use on pages 146–7. We were also helped by Ann Jeavons, Adèle Greene, Dick Mayon-White, Peter Morris, David Weatherall, Harriet Sansom, Mary Marzillier, Colin Blakemore, Richard Peto and John Galway. We are grateful to the Family Planning Association for providing the leaflet which forms the basis of pages 64–73.

To all these people, and the many others who have helped us in the preparation of both books, we would like to say THANK YOU.

Ann McPherson and Aidan Macfarlane

Contents

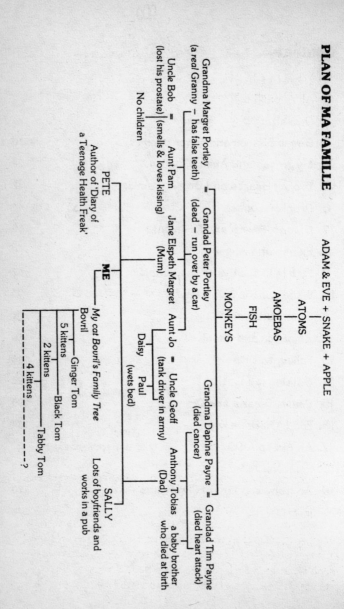

All About **Me**

Dear Marie Cerveau,

I am writing to you because mon school says you are my Exchange Français. Je hope to make cette exchange par train via le Channel Tunnel n'est ce pas? Avez vous peur de travelling dans un tunnel sub la mer?

I thought peut être vous might like to know quelque chose about moi and ma famille. I hope you will write and tell me quelque chose about you.

Ma nom is Susie. J'ai nearly 16 ans et my birthday est January 16th. Mes eyes sont grey/brown et ma hair est long et aussi brownish and une terrible mess. Je n'aime pas school much because je think the teachers sont boring but je ne suis pas mal at biology and pas assez good at French.

1

I habite in a maison in London. It is ne pas very jolie. But I love it and it has un bon garden. Ma famille est mon père, ma mère, mon older frère et ma older sister et sa chat—Bovril. But now she is ma chat because Sally never gives her un repas. J'aime ma chat beaucoup. Je have done un arbre of my family which I am sending with this letter so vous can understand my family better.

In my maison there are:

First mon frère Pete who is très clever and un grand pain in the butt. He is 17 ans et un 'groff', and toujour gets le 'A*'s in his examinations. He has un place a Nottingham University to do medicin. He is un étudiant de 'driving' but is très mal at that. He is aussi un 'Health Freak' and pense toujours of his body and writes about it dans son diary. I think qu'il est un hypochondriac. Do you have these in France too? Il aime the alcohol but mum ne knows pas. He is also always trying to get off with les girls but is not very bon at it. He used to have une girlfriend qui s'appelle Cilla though now she is, how do you say? passant? He has un très joli ami who is called Sam, whom all the girls aiment beaucoup et me also, but he just thinks of me as Pete's petite sister. Aussi Pete teases me all the time and calls me 'stupide', though I am not, but I get my own back about his glasses. He takes them off when he veut to be a bit more sexy. When you are here, prenez le care when he takes his glasses off!

Ma sister Sally a 21 years. She is très difficile et un rebel. Mum worries about elle all the time and shouts. She habite with her latest boyfriend who nobody here aimes much. Elle est très, très, très pretty and I wish I looked like her. She goes to beaucoup de parties and spends tout her time at le pub where she works. She used to be a chevaux or should it be cheveux (anyhow a hair) dresser. Je ne sais pas which.

Mon père has a gros stomach and is almost bald. He is gentil but his travail is not very gentil. He is a 'Killer de Pestes'. He has quelque chose which he calls a moustache. Il s'appelle Tony et il smokes cigarettes and pretends il doesn't.

Next is ma mère. She is très bossy and interfering but I think you will really aime her because she is très jolie and funny. Elle mange too much and aime beaucoup le chocolat. Elle s'appelle Jane et elle est a bit grosse everywhere but pretends she isn't. I worry about getting grosse like her. She always wants to know quelque choses about what I am doing and where I am going and avec who. Sometimes she has the same colour hair as moi but it's curly.

Je want to visite EuroDisney, but ma mère ne want pas me to, parce ce que elle thinks that I will pas learn beaucoup de French there and elle n'aime pas Monsieur Mickey Mouse.

Mes amies are Kate, Emma, Sita, Sheila and sometimes Mary. Le music que nous aimons beaucoup is Oasis, Blur and Sting and nous aimons aller à la Disco aussi, mais ma mère ne know pas about this. My plus close friend who really understands me is Bovril—ma chat—who also aime les boys très much and is always avec them and having kittens.

J'aime les sports, comme swimming and running, and je suis in the school team, but also j'ai hayfever. I hate ma face as it keeps getting les spots and I have to cover it with le make-up which we can't wear at school.

I hope you like my French—please write about yourself and what 'group' you like beaucoup. Do you keep a diary? Je keep a très special book into which I stick everything.

Your exchange amie,

Susie

P.S. Je n'aime pas meat and when I come and stay with you can I just mange vegetables please? Je pense that it is cruel and horrid to kill les animals.

P.P.S. Joke:

Question: Why does mon frère Pete, who trouve his body si intéressant, wear his underpants in the shower?

Answer: Because il n'aime pas regarder the unemployed.

3

Organizing
Boys, Sex and **Work**

1st January

I love new diaries. All clean and delicious. Waiting to be written on.

Pete thinks I'm being a copycat, still keeping a diary when his is so famous. He's been dead moody since Cilla went off with David. Anyhow Pete's not the only person in the world keeping a diary. Unlike him, I'm going to write everything that I can think of down, exactly as it happens. If I write something wrong then it'll be like telling lies to myself. That's why I hope this one'll be secret.

2nd January

Only fourteen days to my birthday. Can't wait till I'm 16 when I'll be able to:

* get married with the consent of Mum or Dad (Pete would be delighted to get rid of me)

* leave school and get a full-time job
* leave home with the consent of Mum or Dad (Bovril would have to come too)
* choose my own doctor and decide on my own medical treatment
* have my own driving licence for moped or motorcycle (not that Mum would let me)
* buy a lottery ticket
* buy cigarettes (at least now it's legal)
* have sexual intercourse (mmmmmmh)
* get an abortion without Mum or Dad's consent (no way)
* buy premium bonds (already got some from Aunty Jo)
* drink alcohol in a hotel, but only if I'm having a meal (no drinking with Sal down the pub yet).

  But I still must have Mum or Dad with me if I'm interviewed by the police (hope this never happens!).

  I've got to wait till I'm 17 before I can:
* gamble or go into a betting shop, but I can't make a bet till I'm 18
* join the armed forces, though Mum and Dad still have to approve
* get a regular driving licence for cars but not for heavy lorries
* go to prison.

  But I'm jealous that Pete, this year, when he's 18, can:
* see an '18' film
* get a cheque book and credit card
* vote (maybe when I can vote I'll help change the government)
* apply for a mortgage
* buy alcohol in a pub and drink it there
* give blood (yugh)
* leave home, live with whoever he wants to, and get married without consent (won't be to Cilla, that's for sure)
* change his name without Mum and Dad's consent
* see his birth certificate, even if he's adopted
* be a member of a jury
* get his own passport without Mum or Dad's signature.

3rd January

Pete's sex mad. Seems to be already thinking of trying to put his 'medical knowledge' into practice. He's got a book out of the library about human behaviour. It has a bit about why people are attracted to one another. I'm sure it's all just about sex, but he says it's 'useful stuff' knowing how people choose mates.

He says it all happens by 'sexual sequencing'. When you meet someone at a party or something, whether you are first attracted to them or not probably just depends on looks and ways of dressing (but Pete says it's probably smells like pheromones, as well). After that a kind of game begins which is stopped if one or the other person doesn't want to go on. Pete said the problem was when one person wanted to go on and the other didn't—like him and Cilla.

His book says the 'courtship game' (sounds like something in ancient history) starts with looking at each other's bodies (the 'looking stage'), then gazing into each other's eyes. Then comes the 'talking stage' when you are finding out about one another; then a bit of touching, not the proper stuff but sort of disguised, helping you off with your coat, or taking your hand to help you across a road. Next, a bit more touching, like your bodies coming into closer contact, brushing against one another as if by accident. Things get to a slightly more intimate bit when you actually hold hands. Then comes the great leap to the kiss, followed by more serious touching and fumbling. Pete said I was too young to hear the next stages as they were classified '18'.

Mum says Pete's got a one-track mind and that he ought to go and talk to the family doctor about it. Pete said, 'Hope she's got all afternoon.' I told Mum it was normal. Mizz says the average male thinks of sex every eight minutes, and as I reckon Pete thinks about it every two minutes, she shouldn't worry as he's got it sorted.

4th January

Can't keep up. Pete's lost Cilla and now fancies Sandy. But Sandy fancies Sam, so Pete's been trying to go out with Brenda, who will go out with anyone. However, Sam's going out with Joanna, so Sandy's going out with Randy Jo, who actually fancies Emma.

I fancy Sam and Pete says he likes me, but he never does anything about it. I am gasping to go out with him and he's on my mind all the time. I wish I could speak to him but I can't. Maybe I'll never find anyone to go out with and I'll die an old maid.

5th January

Not a good way of starting the first weekend of the New Year—sitting here, fed up with work and not getting anything done.

Pete's admitted to me he's tried cannabis! (I'm putting it in my blackmail book for when he gets difficult.) Said it was last year—with Cilla. Asked him why it was OK to smoke cannabis but not cigarettes. He said it wasn't OK at all. At the time he'd thought it was harmless but he'd found out that smoking a few cannabis cigarettes had the same bad effects on your lungs as smoking more than twenty normal cigarettes, and it wasn't any better for your brain. I wouldn't touch them—they screw your life up, and the people who sell drugs to children should be hanged.

6th January

Every time I sit down to start revising for my mock GCSEs, I panic. I get this awful sick feeling in my stomach and rush off to the toilet. Then I make myself another cup of coffee. How does Pete do it? His room looks and smells like the local council tip, his love life's a mess, his spots are like lunar craters and ten times worse than mine, but he has got his work organized. I just flit from book to book—from maths to biology, French to history, physics to English lit and lang— getting absolutely nothing done. Eight subjects seems laughable. At least I managed to finish some of the coursework. Mocks in two weeks—should have worked in the Christmas holidays like boring Mum kept on and on to me about. Don't know why it makes me furious, her always being right. Not that I'd let her know.

But anyhow, who works at Christmas? No way I'd miss the parties, plus my friends wanting presents which were 'just right'. Multicoloured boxer shorts from the Sock Shop for guess who (S . .). Mum and Dad are the worst. It's 'Anything you've made would be lovely.' Why can't they be the same as everybody else and like what I buy them? Got Dad a pair of boxer shorts too—really with-it. He said they were just what he wanted, then I found them in the Oxfam pile on New Year's Day. (Not sure what a Third World flood victim would make of them—use them for holding up his house?) Got bright scarlet frilly knickers for Mum, to jazz up her sex life—but think Pete's now got them at the bottom of his wardrobe with his porno mags—they're like teenage mags, but everyone has all their clothes off.

7th January

Can't concentrate. My mind keeps coming back to everything I should be doing and still can't—and Sam. I'm a world-class expert in excuses—got to ring my friends to find out what they're doing, got to clean my room (even that's better than working), got to find my blue, crippled 'chewed to nothing' pen. I've got five, but it's the only one that feels right and it's been lost for a week. Worst thing is I've fallen out of love with Bovril. She shat on my bed last night—Mum made me clear it up which made me puke.

Think I'll make a list of suitable boys for me to love:

John—8/10—passable, not a bad kisser (once at Christmas), lives three doors away, in my class, a bit juvenile, still into Goth, think he dyes his hair, farts a lot—don't think I could live with so much smell.
Sam—10/10—desirable but doesn't seem to know I even exist. Pete's best friend, self-confident but not a poser. His dad's a leader too—a medical scientist—an Immu . . . something.
Ram—7/10—Sita's older brother. Really attractive but a bit shy.
Mark—2/10—sad. Sixth-former and a nobody boy—I'd rather go out with his 7-year-old brother.
Andrew—5/10—OK but in my year. Big-headed—tries it on with all the girls—even me. Smells of fags and wears white socks.
Winston—8/10—very fit and athletic.
Mike—the midget. Nice, friendly but doesn't really score as he seems to prefer boys.

8th January
Back at school. I never want to look at a French book again.

Resolution: not to be late any more.

Drama looks great. I'm acting being a paralysed girl after a car accident.

9th January
Revision. It's no good, it won't go away. Kate's for coasting along and then slaving for three weeks before exams. Can't muck about with GCSE though—so much depends on the teacher's opinion.

Still hiding my last term's report from Mum and Dad. What some of them have written is not brilliant to say the least. Typical Mum asked where it was. I said the school had decided not to give them out.

REPORT

English

Not good — though she could be if she spent more time in class concentrating on her work and less talking to her friends. She also has irritating lapses of attention in class.

J. Jensen.

Physics

Oh dear — Susie not only doesn't do her own work properly but she distracts others as well. I have no idea whether she is any good at this subject. Her homework is always late and when it is handed in it has more to do with flights of fancy than with fact. Having catpaw marks all over it doesn't help its legibility. O. Boil

Biology

Susie could do very well in her GCSE and might even manage an 'A'. However she must continue to work hard, right up to the examinations, to achieve this. She seems to have a particular interest in the workings of the human body. I wish her luck.

N. Smellie

Chemistry

Good at experimenting but not always with the ingredients she's meant to. V. Singh.

French

Susie has not kept up her interest in this subject. Her efforts to do absolutely nothing have paid off.

G. Dunsop

History

This is a confident, if rather over-gregarious young lady. Her essays, though informative, are rather slapdash. She needs to improve the organization of her study periods and homework. Recent history and discussion are her strong points. Trextring

Maths

Susie's performance is difficult to judge, as she has been away for a great many lessons this term. Much work is needed. When she is present, she tends to blow hot and cold, having periods of extreme activity followed by periods of quiet relaxation. P. Pie.

Drama

She obviously enjoys the subject. Sometimes goes a bit 'over the top'. She should do well.
G. Smiles

P.E.

She has great ability but prefers not to use it.

K. Court

Form Teacher's Report

There are certainly some strengths here, and Susie is a most likeable person, BUT... she'll have to try harder. I think it would help if you would come and discuss this report with me please. Susie needs to improve her working methods if she is ever to succeed to the best of her abilities. M. Rogers.

Head's Report

Patchy and rather disappointing. I feel that Susie could really do better. Her behaviour has not always been as good as it might have been either.
I. MacIntosh

I think there must be a special book of clichés for teachers to use in school reports. It probably has translations as well, like:

'could do better if she tried' = 'totally hopeless'
'has great potential' = 'maybe but I've never seen it'
'outstanding work' = 'never turns up with homework'
'contributes well to discussions' = 'never stops talking'
'must beware of complacency' = 'bone idle'
'must apply herself better' = 'applying herself to work rather than flirting with boys might just help'.

Anyhow, I've decided I'm going to get French GCSE, become Prime Minister, and put the education system back together again. Lucky about outside moderators, but I'm not sure how much it will help. Don't know whether schools are for passing exams, for learning facts, for keeping teachers off the streets, or for looking good in the school league tables.

10th January

Even writing to smelly old Aunty Pam and embarrassing and prostateless Uncle Bob is better than working. I put:

> Dear Aunty Pam and Uncle Bob
> It was lovely seeing you at Christmas. Thank you for the lovely present and delicious lunch. The present was just what I wanted. How are you? I hope you are both well.
> Thank you again . . .

Couldn't think of anything else. Certainly wasn't going to tell them about my non-existent social life. Uncle Bob's been on at me about my boyfriends since I was 6. It only filled four lines. Couldn't even remember if they'd given me tights or a scarf—both day-glow pink which is what confused me. More for the Oxfam pile. There will be a very hot person in Africa wearing pink tights, a pink scarf, and boxer shorts with 'hard stuff' written across them. Bet Mum insists I wear their present when we next visit. She'll go on about hurting Aunty Pam's 'feelings'. What about my feelings? Being made to look a twat. Don't think Sam, or anyone else, would fancy me if they saw me in day-glow pink.

At least Aunty Jo's better at presents. Money—just what I wanted. Mum thought it was very generous as she's having a bad time in Germany.

11th January

Forgot what the homework was that had to be in tomorrow. Phoned all my friends. Panic made worse—they'd all already done it. Kate and Sita had even gone off to the shops. Never asked me did they? I just can't cope—but Mum said she'd help sort it out. Anyhow Mary told me that John is going to chuck Kate. Says she's 'a slag'. He's one to talk.

Another thing I hate is favouritism from the teachers. I turn up in a mini-skirt and get 'Why are you wearing a postage stamp to school?'. Kate does the same and is praised for looking attractive.

Susie's Birthday List

New body (top!) or brain—or just new clothes
CD player
HMV music token (so I can buy my own CD and not one that Pete wants)
Beatles 1969–70 CD
New bike
Oil burner with cinnamon oil
Obsession perfume
 Marc Chagall poster
Hand-made clay Peruvian men
Jilly Cooper books
Arty calendar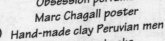
Filofax organizer
Nice ear-rings
One-way ticket to Australia in case I fail my GCSEs
My own mobile—so I can always chat without any hassle

List of birthday presents I'll leave around for everybody to see.

12th January

Pete's in a sulk. Shouted at me for using the rest of his zit cream. Says he needs it more than me. Told him that men with pits on their face are great—like Mark Owen of Take That. Noticed Pete had this great graze on his cheek between the spots. He was furious I'd noticed. Sam and him had been riding Sam's new motorbike and had skidded on a bend. Luckily they'd been wearing crash helmets and the bike was only slightly bent. Pete said he'd kill me if I said anything to Mum or Dad. More blackmail material for the future.

13th January

Mrs Smith, who lives two doors away, is giving me some tips

on how to sort out my work. Turns out she used to be a teacher. This week we're concentrating on:

Organizing your room and your table

1 MAKE SURE THE LIGHT IS RIGHT—
I'm to ask Mum to get me a new one that shines downwards.

2 CLEAR THE TABLE YOU USE AS A DESK—
this took ages as I kept finding things that I thought I'd lost.

3 PUT ALL THE STUFF ON DIFFERENT SUBJECTS INTO SEPARATE, MARKED FILES—
luckily Pete had some left over. He eventually managed to give me six. I sometimes think he doesn't want me to do well.

4 GET PAPER, PENS AND PENCILS—
had these already but put them neatly together where I could find them.

5 GET RID OF DISTRACTIONS—
Mrs S said that music's OK—so have recorded the latest Sting album on tape for my headphones.

It's unbelievable—Mark (he only gets 1/10 now) is going out with a year 8—baby snatching. She's not only ugly with no sign of tits but is stupid as well. He's got no taste, which is why I don't fancy him. One thing about having a birthday and growing up—it makes you feel really embarrassed looking back at when you were 13 or 14. Especially reading my old diaries. I can't believe the things I wrote. Absolutely cringe at what I wore, who I fancied, and who was my idol. Started to think, yugh—will I look back when I'm 18 or 19 and be horrified about what I am like now?

Sweet Sixteen and I've Never…

16th January

MY BIRTHDAY!

MY BIRTHDAY!!

MY BIRTHDAY!!!

MY BIRTHDAY!!!!

MY BIRTHDAY!!!

Nice not being at school on my birthday. Was sure nobody would have remembered. Pete's first words to me were, 'Just because you've reached the age of consent doesn't mean you've got to say yes.' Sam won't remember. He's still going out with Joanna. I pretend I don't mind because I really like her, but it actually makes me totally miserable. Don't think anyone likes me. And nobody remembers Christmas and birthdays if they come together. Mum and Dad could have been a bit more thoughtful when they decided to do it.

Some of the time Mum really does my head in—fuss, fuss, fuss—but sometimes she's wonderful. Gave me a 'surprise' tea party. Kate, Sita and Emma all came round. Why couldn't Pete have invited S? He invited Randy Jo instead. Even Sally came, skived off work. I'm sure she'll get the sack. Miss her not being at home.

My Presents: ❋❋❋❋❋❋❋❋❋❋❋❋❋❋

Mum—new body (but no new brain) and a Tom Cruise poster—brilliant

Dad—second-hand bike to replace the one stolen last month (not surprising as I was riding his all the time), plus a crash helmet which I could have done without

Pete—forgot *again*—that makes six birthdays and four Christmases in a row. So he promised to get me a National Lottery ticket. Told him I wanted 01 02 03 04 05 06

Sal—make-up paintbox (slightly used?), perfume and an invite to the pub

Emma—three Jilly Cooper books

Kate—compilation tape she made up herself—can't wait to see what's on it

Sita—Indian ear-rings—OK!

Randy Jo—forgot, though I suspect it was him who donated a couple of gas releases during tea

Bovril—think she's been at it again, so it will have to be kittens

---

17th January

Letter from Charlotte who used to be in my class at school and one of our group. We competed against one another in running—till her dad got a job in Birmingham.

My reply!

The cheek of it—your letter arrived dated the 16th, I repeat the 16th. What happens on this wondrous day? Yep, it is National Holiday to the world, in other words Susie's birthday. So I open your letter expecting . . . a pop-up box of chocolates? a National Lottery ticket? or even (sigh) a little birthday card? What do I find? A measly old bumbly letter with NO happy birthday messages. No presents. No wishes—just absolutely nothing but news of YOU and how much happier you are up there now that your dad's got a job! Enough complaining. Actually I loved getting it, and I LOVE getting letters, even if I can't read your writing. I don't suppose it's my fault I'm dyslexic, or your fault you're dysgraphic—just our parents' and our schools'.
Love . . . your very grown-up friend . . . Susie.

P.S. Have you DONE IT yet?

18th January

Pete's pathetic—a tiny cold and he thinks he's dying. Moan, moan, moan. But as soon as Mum told him there was a letter for him, he leapt out of bed and rushed downstairs. Letter was from the library—five books overdue by a month. I nearly fell downstairs laughing. Pete says I'm basically an unsympathetic person and that I never believe him when he says he's ill; and if I want any sympathy when I get ill, I'd better not expect it from *him*. Told him everybody gets colds and nobody knows anything about them. Nobody but Dr Pete Payne, BMKA (Bloody Medical Know All), that is.

Even if he had yesterday off, he hadn't wasted his time.

He's written an article for the school newspaper where he's doing a weekly column on health. This week—his own problem—colds. Next week it's hayfever (my problem), then skin problems, asthma, headaches, sex and contraception, throwing-up and the runs. He's asked me to write the one on sex and contraception as he thought I ought to learn about it now I'm 16, if I didn't know it all already. He gave me his 'Colds' piece to read as an example of the kind of thing he wants. He doesn't credit me with a mind.

Colds, Coughs and Vitamin C

On average we get between one and five colds a year, though my sister seems to have one all the time. (She claims it's hayfever, which I have to agree is caused by something different.)

Colds are caused by viruses called Rhino viruses (Rhino meaning nose or nostril, like Rhinoceroses which are named after their big horns.) There are loads of different types of these viruses and our bodies are not much good at fighting them off, which is why we get loads of colds.

These viruses are spread in the sprays from our coughs and sneezes more than by poking our fingers up our noses to get at our snot. (You still shouldn't do that, or at least not where your friends can see, and as for eating it afterwards—a disgusting habit, even if it does taste good, but don't ask me how I know.)

So why do all us horrible people get snotty and drippy when we have a cold? Well, there are these tiny glands in our noses

---

which make the sticky stuff that mixes with all the nasty things that get up our noses—like our fingers, dust, other dirt, and bacteria—to make up our very own personal snot. All this then gets mixed up with our nose hairs (yes, we all have them, not just those wrinklies out there—though theirs are more obvious and foul).

This lovely mixture of viruses, snot, and so on stirs everything up, and what with blowing your nose—no, sorry, forget that—wiping your nose on your sleeve, or sniffing and swallowing the gunk, everything around and in your nose gets nicely red and sore.

Another fact: although colds are commoner in the winter, just *getting* cold doesn't seem to make you more likely to get 'a cold'. That's what the research shows anyway. It also shows that kissing someone with a cold doesn't mean that the other person will get a cold, as long as the one with the cold doesn't breathe or sneeze—so keep up the good work all those having a kissing 'sesh' out there (and practise kissing without breathing!).

Because they are caused by viruses, antibiotics don't do anything towards curing colds, so it's probably better just to use something that makes you 'feel' better, like paracetamol, hot drinks, and tender loving care from someone who loves you, should you be so lucky (definitely not my sister).

Although drug companies spend millions of pounds trying to advertise 'cold cures', there *is* nothing that 'cures' colds, although something to dry up your snot may make you feel happier.

And as for Vitamin C, well, you can try it, even if none of the experiments so far show it actually works.

I'll never forgive him—telling the whole school. I threw his mug of last week's coffee at him that he'd been growing new and disgusting strains of fungal penicillin on—and yelled that it was him who said it wouldn't make any difference to his cold—getting soaking wet and having antibiotics. Dad was furious, because it did make a difference to the carpet.

Anyhow, I was interested in what he said about Vitamin C. We'd just done that in school and I thought it cured something called 'scurvy' when your gums bleed and your teeth all drop out. Mrs Smellie said they'd done an experiment on sailors with scurvy in the eighteenth century and had tried giving different groups of sailors cider, sulphuric acid, vinegar, sea water, mustard, two oranges and two lemons, and a ship's normal diet. We were being taught about 'controls', and the question was whether this was a controlled experiment. I said no—but Pete said that I'd got it wrong—the ship's normal diet was the 'control'. He explained that without having one group of sailors who didn't have anything extra they wouldn't have been able to tell whether the sailors had just got better with time alone. Anyhow, this experiment showed that the sailors who had the oranges and lemons got better and the sailors who had the other things or nothing didn't. It wasn't until a hundred years later they knew it was Vitamin C in the oranges and lemons that had done it. Maybe Vitamin C will be found to stop colds in another hundred years.

19th January
Mocks have started—no comment.

20th January
Mum has had a nightmare that the librarians from the local library are out to kill her. She dreamt they were stationed with guns at every window and door of the house, with no escape. They were chanting 'bring back the books, bring back the books' and 'pay your fines, pay your fines'. No more driving lessons till Pete takes his books back. Mum thinks it's really mean on the other people wanting the books. Pete said he'd return the books but dream interpretation was rubbish. He'd had a dream about being chased while naked and riding a burning horse down a long corridor full of people.

Makes me almost believe that dreams are kinds of messages—I'm sometimes dreaming about a fire engine when I'm woken up by my alarm bell. No one seems to know whether dreams are just a waste disposal machine for unwanted thoughts, or whether they are DEEPLY meaningful. One of Pete's unreturned books was on the interpretation of dreams. It fell open at the appropriate page so he must have been reading it.

Being chased—dreamers want to escape from someone. The person chasing them can also represent some aspect of the dreamer that they are unhappy with.

Riding—a fairly obvious sexual symbol, though there is commonly fear as well as desire.

Nakedness—depending on circumstances, and on whether the dreamers are embarrassed and the crowd takes any notice, this can mean inferiority, inadequacy or, alternatively, a desire to be different.

Fire—means passion and danger, and often that thoughts about sex are causing trouble.

Corridor—a feeling that you want to return to your mother's womb and security.

If this is all true Pete's got problems, but it seems to me that you can interpret dreams any way you want to, like the stars.

23rd January

Speechless—FIVE of my national lottery numbers came up
..........! There it was in the paper! I'd won £100,000! More
money than I'd ever dreamed of. I could get all the birthday
presents I missed out on, plus a stereo hi fi and a ticket to
Australia!

I pitched into Pete's room without knocking. He did not look
pleased. 'My ticket, my ticket—give it me, give it me—I've
won,' I screamed. Blank puzzled stare. 'What are you talking
about?' I could only scream, 'My ticket, my ticket,' on and on
and on.

The bastard hadn't even bought it. I held his pillow over his
face, but he was too strong.

Louise was doing art though now maybe she's not. She's
having second thoughts as she was crucified by Mrs Saicops,
her art teacher. Sometimes teachers can be really cruel. She
said that some pupils have application and no talent but
they'll probably do all right, but that Louise has neither
application nor talent. I think this is shitty and not even true.
It's straight-up bitchiness because Mrs Saicops doesn't like
Louise. No knowledge of psychology these teachers. If I'm told
I'm bad at something, it makes me mad, and I become bad at
it so as to fit in with what the teachers think. Louise was so
upset she was crying.

Teachers bullying are bad enough—other kids even worse.
Some people seem to attract it, especially those who don't
know how to stick up for themselves. We talked about it on
the school council and we're drawing up a code to try to stop
it. Sometimes it's just people being rude to one another like
saying, 'Your mum's a tart, I wouldn't fancy sleeping with her',
and at other times it's real physical stuff with several boys
picking on one who sticks out for some reason.

Still can't believe about the lottery ticket. Some people go
mad when they think they've won and they haven't—why did I
trust Pete?

My Writes
and **Animal Rights**

4

27th January

Louise's dad had it out with Mrs Saicops about art. Glad it wasn't my dad. I'd be acutely grieved—but it worked. Mrs Saicops praised her last life drawing—creep.

Dad kept asking me questions, just as all Pete's friends were arriving to watch the big match. Mark and Sam came with Randy Jo. Dad talked but I didn't listen, and he left in a peck.

I changed into 501s and my new body. It's a bit clingy, so I changed out again. Can't see myself wearing it in public—despite Mum nagging I've never worn it.

Football's boring—I don't know who anyone is. Wrongly thought I was supporting Sam's team. Made some remarks about Joanna—weren't all nice, weren't all nasty. One advantage of older brothers—they do have friends.

29th January

Mocks have finished—still no comment!

3rd February

Note from Mrs Smith about keeping up with my work plans.
Want to watch telly—great programme about snakes mating.
Have to miss it though—got to work.

Organizing Your Subjects

1 Write a list of all the subjects you are doing.
2 List them from the ones that you know least about to the ones you know best.
3 Then list for each subject all the bits of that subject you should know.
4 Keep each subject in its folder to stop them from getting muddled up.
5 Get a diary and work out how many days and hours you have for revision before the exams.
6 Work out how much time you have to revise each subject (using simple division!) and write out a programme of work covering all the subjects equally.
7 When you are revising, choose some topics which you already know well and some that you don't, so that you keep feeling OK about it and don't panic or get depressed.

Afraid in my list everything should be top. I'm trying to stop myself panicking, so here goes:

MATHS (no comment)
FRENCH ('orrible)
COMBINED SCIENCE
    PHYSICS (great but difficult, and awful teacher)
    CHEMISTRY (the sexual kind—preferably)
    BIOLOGY (the real facts!)
ENGLISH (sort of OK)
ENGLISH LIT (OK)
HISTORY (more OK)
DRAMA (comes naturally to me)

Fed up with work, there must be more to life than this. But Mrs Smith says 'the more you can do today, the less you need to do tomorrow'—and that working will make me feel less anxious.

Can't find my French book—not that I really looked. My biology list looks like this:

Life Classifications, Bacteria and Viruses, Fungi, Foods and Feeding.
Green Plant Nutrition, Animal Nutrition, Water Uptake, Blood and Lymphatic System, Respiration, Excretion.
Temperature Regulation, Sensitivity, Co-ordination and Response, Support and Locomotion. Reproduction: Plants and Humans, Genes, Evolution, Ecology.

Doesn't seem so bad written out like this. Eighteen topics, say two hours for each. Almost seems possible.

4th February

Want a Valentine's Day party. No chance of Mum saying yes—not after Sally's breaking-up party five years ago!

How does Mum do it? She always knows when I'm lying, like my 'non-existent' school report. She asked me whether Kate and me had been smoking in my room. I said, 'Of course not, Mum. Why do you always pick on me? You know I'd never smoke.' On and on. 'Don't lie to me—I know you have, haven't you?' 'No, honestly Mum, it wasn't me.' Must be the way I answer, or perhaps it's the smell. (How can she smell it through the joss sticks?) She's like an awful firework—we'd just lit up and—bang—she appears out of nowhere. There's no way I'd admit it with £200 at stake from Dad if I don't smoke.

I'm sure I'll die of boredom before lung cancer gets me. The same old lecture. I know it's wrong—she doesn't have to tell me. And it doesn't help, her telling me again and again that

the number of people dying from the effects of smoking is the equivalent of a jumbo jet crashing every day. That it's not just lung cancer that it causes, but heart disease and bronchitis. That once you've started, it's much more difficult to stop. I'm not interested in what's going to happen to me when I'm an old hag in fifty years' time. Anyhow I don't smoke very often, and I'm not going to get addicted, and I wouldn't dream of smoking if I was pregnant. No way I'd want to harm my baby. (Not that I'm going to GET pregnant—I don't even have a boyfriend.)

5th February
Pete wants Bov to be in an animal experiment. He saw this TV programme about a link between two parts of the brain that gives us our sex drive. Seeing Bov at it all the time, he said she'd be ideal to experiment on and for him to look inside her brain. But there might not be anything in there, even if her tummy is full of kittens.

I think it's cruel to do animal experiments, particularly on Bov—after all, she must have feelings. Discussed it with Bov who wasn't much help. I joined an 'Anti Experiments on Animals' group in the 'Animal Rights' phase of my life when I was 14. They said there was no point in testing drugs on animals because humans are different from animals, and some drugs tested OK on animals have been shown to be not safe for humans. As for using animals for making and testing cosmetics—just so you can look beautiful. Nothing will make me beautiful anyhow.

It's so annoying arguing with Pete. I know some of my points are correct but the words just don't come out right. He says I'm only giving a bit of the argument. There have been experiments on animals to do with drugs that are saving *lots* of lives—though Pete agrees that making calves live in crates to make them taste better isn't exactly useful.

But animal experiments were essential in the development of the vaccine which means there is no more smallpox in the world. They were also vital in the development of penicillin and insulin (the medicine used by people with diabetes), and the drugs used to cure childhood leukaemia. Pete had lots more examples, but I didn't want to hear them. He had persuaded me that if the experiments are carefully carried out so as to cause as little suffering as possible, then it's OK.

We both agreed that setting fire to people's houses because they are involved in animal experiments is *mental*, and it's also plain disgusting for girls to plaster their faces with animal products. It doesn't even *look* good.

At the hairdressers I asked whether the stuff she'd put on my hair had been tested on an animal. She said she'd shampooed her cat with it and it seemed OK. Wasn't quite what I'd meant. Maybe the cat was OK afterwards, but I was a mess. Mum asked why I hadn't bothered to brush my hair today.

8th February

At last—my French Exchange has written. Not that she said much. Her letter was rather formal. All she said was, 'Thank you for your letter. I'll tell you all about myself when you come to Paris. See you soon, Marie Cerveau.' In French. Managed to translate it with the aid of my dictionary (found in Pete's room). Funny, I used to be really good at translating French when I was in France, two years ago.

At last, a birthday present from Pete—a white rabbit with pink eyes. He was given it by Sam, who was given it by his dad, who rescued it from some experiment. Thought of calling it 'Sam', but settled for 'Pinko'. Mum's furious. Says it's going to be her who has to clean it out and feed it, and look after it when it's sick. Don't actually like it much. Don't fancy its pathetic pink eyes.

9th February
NOBODY, NOBODY noticed my new haircut. So much for £29 and for friends.

Started revising BACTERIA AND VIRUSES. To help me remember, I made lots of little notes and stuck them all over the house, above my bed, in the toilet, on the back of the hall door.

Rubella:
1) Also known as German Measles
2) Caused by a virus
3) Harmless to person who catches it
4) Very harmful to baby if you catch it when pregnant
5) Can be prevented by having an immunization against it
6) Everyone should be immunized, when they are 1 year old.

Chlamydia:
1) Caused by a bacteria
2) Gives a discharge from the penis or vagina, pain on peeing, but sometimes no symptoms at all in the early stages
3) Can make you sterile (not able to have babies)
4) Easily treated with an antibiotic
5) Quite common in men and women
6) Condoms reduce the chances of catching it.

Pete stuck up a notice saying, 'If you think you've got a sexually transmitted disease, Chlamydia or any other, your local GU (Genito-Urinary) clinic number is . . . . . '. Mum went spare—notes about French verbs all over the house is one thing, notes about sexually transmitted diseases is another. Wasn't having her house turned into a public toilet, 'Thank you very much.' Can't understand it—it's only my revision.

Pete's in Mum's bad books anyway. He missed a driving lesson last night—the last one before his test. I made things better by telling Mum how many people had probably survived as a result. Pete's not amused. He thinks I'm joking, but while he's learning, I'm on the most efficient but dangerous form of transport known—my bike.

I remember when Pete had his accident a couple of years ago. He had a long lecture from the doctor about how 200 people a year get killed and 24,000 injured on bikes each year, and saying that cycle and motorcycle accidents are the commonest cause of death in young people. Pete's never worn a crash helmet since, and neither have I, but we both know we should. I'd look such a nerd with Dad's white plastic bowl of a birthday present on my head. I think it's stupid that there's not a law about it. Then I'd have to wear one, and so would everyone else, and we'd all look nerds and I wouldn't stand out.

10th February
Got my own passport from the post office today. Ghastly photo—makes me look like Dad. Now I know I'm not adopted. What a way to find out.

Broken **Hearts**
and *Broken* **Families**

12th February
Pete failed his driving test today. Damaged his ego, especially
as Sam's passed (hurrah). Also damaged his driving
instructor's car.

We're about to have a German invasion. Uncle Geoff, who's
married to Aunty Jo (Mum's sister who doesn't smell), has
gone off with 'another woman'. Aunty Jo can't stand being by
herself any longer, so she's coming over for a bit of sympathy
from Mum. Can't see why anyone would go off with an alcoholic,
curly-headed, midget ex-British Army tank driver like Uncle
Geoff. Would have to be even more desperate than me—
though Pete thinks that even I won't have any trouble. There
are 3 per cent more boys than girls around nowadays, and by
the year 2025 there will be 105 men to every 100 women.

If Dad left Mum for another woman Pete said he'd go to the trouble of doing him over.

It's quite out of order—I have to share my bedroom with my cousin Daisy. I know I don't particularly like the name 'Susie'—but Daisy! Daisy was a 9-year-old prat the last time I saw her. I hated her, and her 5-year-old brother, Paul, who used to wet his bed. Always knew because he never got up in the same colour pyjamas he went to bed in. Mum said his bed-wetting was because his bladder wasn't mature yet. Like the rest of him, I'd say. He'd got better with some kind of alarm thing in his bed that woke him up when he peed. He used to tell Pete how he'd dream about wanting to pee in his sleep, and then he'd wake up and find he'd done it in his bed. Got my own back on Mum about not being able to use the phone. She's on to her sister in Germany every day. One day Uncle Geoff's gone, the next he's back.

Couldn't bear it if Mum and Dad separated. Suppose you never know though. Even the Royals are doing it and their kids look absolutely miserable. I'm sure that I'll never get divorced—doubt whether I'll even get the chance. If it did happen to Mum and Dad, I don't think I would be able to speak about it. Hardest thing would be deciding who to go with. I wouldn't want to hurt either of them and make them think I didn't love them as much. Would be specially bad at celebrations and Christmas and things—having to choose. Some things might be better, like I could get twice as much pocket-money. Also I could be with Dad when I wanted to stay out late and didn't want to be hassled about work, and with Mum when I wanted money for clothes. (Dad still can't see why I can't make do with Sal's old clothes. Can't expect him to know anything about 'fashion' in his old M & S suit bought by Mum.)

Kate's parents divorced when she was 4. She couldn't understand why her father went. She's never really forgiven him for what he did to her mum. It was dreadful. Grown-ups are really inconsiderate and selfish. They just think of themselves. But actually I can't imagine myself ever finding someone I'd want to spend all my life with. Certainly no one I know now—not even Sam. Kate stayed with her mum living off social security and always short of money. She doesn't think people understand how bad it is for the children—they're just treated like a statistic. One in three marriages ends in divorce. It was when Kate went through a bad patch at school recently that she felt she needed her dad most.

13th February
Don't feel like writing today. Totally PISSED OFF.

14th February
VALENTINE'S DAY. NO PARTY, NO CARDS, NO RED ROSES.

My Valentine's Day has been as romantic as a day's outing to Aunty Pam's.

Pete got three cards and waved them under my nose when I got home. He said I could have them second hand if I wanted. I asked him where his fatal charm comes from—with his pebble eyes. Never see it myself. He probably wrote them all himself. Did my moan bit to Mum about having a party. Think she's cracking.

15th February
Two day-late Valentine cards! One's definitely from Mum. Can tell from the innocent smile on her face and the exclamations of 'I wonder who it can be from?' and (from Dad) 'Who's the secret admirer then?'. The other one—I hope it's Sam, it must be Sam, let it be Sam. Sam, Sam, is it you?

16th February
It was Sam—Pete made him do it. Totally embarrassed.

19th February
A week off school.

20th February
Daisy and her brother Paul arrive tomorrow—yugh. What a way to spend half-term. Lecture from Mum about being 'nice to poor Daisy'. Lecture from Pete about girls being stupider than boys because more of them are smoking nowadays and anyway they have smaller brains. Told him it is quality not quantity that counts.

21st February
Am writing this sitting on the toilet. Nowhere else is private. Daisy doesn't seem very upset to me. Just interested in commenting on everything in my room.

22nd February

Daisy's a pain. Must be awful for her, but it's tough always being nice to someone you don't like, even if they are having a hard time. She hasn't improved with the years. Aunty Jo's really nice. She's in Sal's old room. Pity it's so small. Daisy and the thing called her brother must have their father's PPP (Pissing, Poor, Protoplasmic) genes. My biology revision has not been in vain. I also got an A— for my test on bacteria. Paul's sleeping in Pete's room. Pete is none too pleased, especially as Paul wet the bed last night. Just got up and turned the mattress over to try and hide it. Didn't hide the smell.

Got it from Mum that Paul's bed-wetting had started again when Uncle Geoff left. This didn't impress Pete who said he'd go to Sam's if it went on. I offered to go instead. Pete said no way would Sam be interested in MY body. Mum said she hoped there's no way Sam would be interested in his. Pete was not amused. Seems to have lost his sense of humour. Mum said later that all boys worried about being homosexual sometime. I think he's depressed—Brenda not responding to his charms and not impressed by him failing his driving test.

Pete likes teasing as long as it's not him being teased. When Mum asked him if he wanted anything from Sainsbury's he said, 'Yes—some sanity please.' Bov's the only one who understands how I feel about S. If Mum and Dad separated, I'd take Bov—whoever I went with.

23rd February

It's like old times. Charlotte's down from Birmingham for the day. It's her half-term too. Great to see her and catch up. Bit strange at first though, seeing if we were the same people as before. Luckily she seemed to get on with Daisy OK. She wanted to know if Daisy missed her friends, specially at times like half-term. Daisy said 'yes'—but that it would be difficult telling them about what had happened, even though a lot of their parents were divorced too. They'd moved around a lot because of her dad's job in the army, which made it difficult to keep friends. But Germany, where her dad was stationed now, was just like England—same shops and everything. And everyone spoke English.

Her dad was very strict when he was at home—which wasn't often. Daisy's sure her mum only married her dad because she was pregnant with her. Sometimes she even wonders whether he really is her dad. Now he's gone off with her mum's best friend, Daisy's pleased that she's with her mum. She said her parents had argued all the time and in some ways she was glad her dad had gone, but she's sure her mum misses him. She was really angry with her mum and dad for not telling her or Paul anything of what was going on.

24th February

Daisy keeps a diary too! Found me writing mine—I forgot to lock the door while peeing and writing. Perhaps I'll get a bit of peace when I go off to Paris.

Big mistake! Gave Mum something I found about 'Having a Party' in a women's magazine Aunty Jo bought. Want to keep the pressure up.

Having a Party

* Limit the numbers you invite by insisting it's by 'invitation only'. If you can run to it, have invitations printed—even very cheaply. Make them instantly recognizable and difficult to copy.
* Take everything down—pictures, and so on. If something can be broken, it will be. Also allow for the fact that the house WILL BE a total wreck afterwards. Cigarette ends get everywhere, as do the pull fasteners to beer cans, and empty beer cans. Even six months later you may still be finding half bottles of whisky stuffed down the back of the sofa. Leave the whole of the next day for clearing up—not just a few hours in the morning. Try arranging for a few hard workers to stay overnight to clean up, but limit numbers to those who are useful.
* Arrange for a couple of boys to be bouncers and pay them to

drink milk all evening. They can keep away gatecrashers. (Gatecrashers are the worst menace—your friends will at least feel faintly ashamed at smashing everything up—gatecrashers feel nothing.) Get the bouncers to throw drunks out before they puke over everything. As back-up—have a parent or some other adult in the house (but not at the party) to help you if things get out of hand.

* Never, never have any of your parents' drink around in the fridge or anywhere else—it will get stolen. It's too embarrassing to search people for hard liquor on the way in so ask them not to bring it. Get them to stick to wine or beer. Try getting your parents and friends to help out with the costs. Wine is preferred and mixing drinks is disastrous. Never have a 'punch'—people will lace it with everything and you'll need to hire an ambulance as well as bouncers.

* Have lots of food—it helps mop up the alcohol. But most people will probably have eaten beforehand. Have things to eat which don't make too much mess. Always have everything disposable—cups, plates, and so on. Have lots of dustbin bags around.

* If you smell cannabis, get the smokers outside on to neutral ground and only allow them back in after they've stopped smoking (thus at least avoiding YOU getting involved with the law). Try having different things going on in different rooms— music, videos, dancing, snogging. Music matters—so it must be good.

* Remember—as host you may have a difficult time at your own party, but it is a long-term investment. Lots and lots of invitations to other people's parties in exchange for short-term hell.

Mum read it and said, 'I'll think about it . . .' I know 'I'll think about it' equals 'No'.

25th February

Pete's turned into a goody-goody. He's just trying to impress—but who cares? He said why didn't I write one of my problem page letters to help Daisy, like I'd written to *Teenage*

Weekly about being fat. Daisy and I wrote it together.

Dear Editor,
I am very depressed and lonely. I thought that my mum and dad were happily married. About a year ago they started arguing and shouting at one another. Dad's gone off with Mum's best friend and I never see him. If Dad can go off I'm afraid that Mum may leave too—and I don't know what will happen to me and my brother. Nobody tells us anything. Daisy—aged 12.

Back to b . . . . y school tomorrow. But a relief to escape Daisy.

3rd March
Pete's now Macho Hero Number One in Daisy's eyes—she thinks he's 'WUUUNDERFUL'. The letter that Daisy and I had written to Teenage Weekly, and a reply, were published.

> ❛It may help you to know you're not alone—so try talking to your friends about it. Each year there are around 175,000 divorces (that means that 350,000 people get divorced). For every two marriages, there is now one divorce. In fact, one in five 16-year-olds have parents who are divorced. In spite of this, a huge study of young people found that they themselves were very optimistic about marriage, and that twenty-nine out of every thirty wanted to get married and twenty-four out of every twenty-five wanted to have children.
>
> One reason for the increase in divorce might be because in previous centuries people lived much shorter lives and would usually have been married for only twenty years or less. Nowadays, with people living to over 70, you may have fifty years or more of married life. No one would pretend that being together for all this time is always easy, and most couples will have some arguments and disagreements from time to time.❜

Other common reasons for parents splitting up are changes in the way people feel about themselves, and changes in their attitudes and in what they mind strongly about. Sometimes people behave in an unacceptable way (sexually or with violence) to the other person, or are unable to cope with children; or they have money problems.

It is very rare for children to want their parents to split up, even if this means the end of arguments, shouting and general confusion. Therefore almost all children feel very sad, and sometimes become bitter and angry with the remaining parent. As parents are caught up in their own anger and upset feelings, the children often feel left out and lonely, and in spite of the fact that it is not their fault at all, may also feel that they are in some way responsible for the break-up.

Try telling your parents that you need to talk to them about what is going on and what is going to happen: where you are going to live, who you are going to live with, what school you are going to go to, where the absent parent is going to live. What young children *don't want* is responsibility for making any of the decisions—like which parent they want to stay with.

One of the best things for separating parents to do is to continue to talk to one another and to their children. They must also realize that their children will continue to love them both, and will want to be reassured of the love of both.

We thought you might like to read about the feelings of some of the other people who have written to us about the same problem.

The thing I am most upset about is my mum leaving when I was 2. I am going through a bad patch at home and school at the moment and it is at times like these that I need my mum badly. My dad is very good though and I am lucky 'cos he is good as a dad and a mum. I needed my mum a while back because I started having fits and it upset my dad. I think my dad misses her as well but he doesn't show it. I am worried that when I do get married and have kids they won't have a gran from my side of the family.

❝ My real parents split up when I was only 3. I was very young and didn't understand. Now I live with an aunt and uncle. My aunt is my father's sister. Not long ago they started fighting really badly and I was afraid they were going to split too. I hate them for what they did to me by bringing me up hating my mum. I don't think people should be allowed to get married until they're sure it's going to work. There should be a probation period so if things don't work out there is no harm done. I also think that if people get a divorce their kids should be allowed to live with one parent or the other. I feel that because of my parents' divorce, if my aunt and uncle divorced I would be the cause of their problems. ❞

❝ My parents have already separated. It was hard at first, but I realize that my parents are probably much happier now. ❞

❝ *About three years ago my parents came very close to separating. The thing that is worst is the violence of it all. There seemed to be such hatred between the two of them. My sisters and I didn't seem to be considered at all. The most horrible thing was going to bed and trying to hide under the quilt and singing to myself so that I couldn't hear all the shouting. All that I wanted to do was to ignore it all and pretend that it wasn't happening. It makes you wonder why they got married in the first place—they seem to have no common interests at all. The problem seems to be a total lack of communication and now this has rubbed off on me and I find it very difficult to talk openly and honestly to people.* ❞

❝ My parents have separated, but they are not divorced yet. It doesn't feel that bad, but it's not like I'm glad he's gone. It's quite the opposite. I see him fairly often but he has just moved quite far away because of work. I can't say I miss him because I still see him. After he had gone I found it hard to tell my friends, even though most of my friends' parents are divorced. I think all my friends know now, but most didn't find out from me. Some did—but only the ones I wanted to know. ❞

❝ I am now fostered after my parents divorced seven years ago. At a younger age, I was very selfish in my views on whose fault it actually was, and 'why did it have to happen to me?' But realizing that I wasn't the only one in this world whose parents have separated, I got on with my life, treating it like a 'fact of life'. It was neither of my parents' fault. In my mind it was just one of those common factors that neither could live with the other any more. Not meaning that they hate each other but just that they had difficulty putting up with one another. Of course I still cry and wish it hadn't happened, but it's now too late to turn the clock back. As far as I am concerned you just have to get on with life, otherwise you don't get anywhere and become one big drop-out!❞

I used to wonder whether I was adopted or something, that maybe Mum and Dad were not my real mum and dad and they had never told me. It's not that I'd mind being adopted. It's just that I'd like to KNOW. I worry about everything, and get myself so worked up I can't sleep. I lie awake until the problem is solved in my mind.

6th March

Drama of the week—Daisy was caught shoplifting at the local Tesco's. Only a very large bar of chocolate. She and Aunty Jo were marched off to the manager, and threatened with the police, but Mum pleaded Daisy needed medical help not prison help. I blame Uncle Geoff. Daisy's been crying ever since, saying it was all an accident. Managed to make her laugh with a joke: 'What's the difference between brussel sprouts and bogies?' Answer: 'You can't get kids to eat brussel sprouts!'

Can't take much more. Thank goodness this German invasion is nearly over. Aunty Jo's been found a temporary army house somewhere, until things are sorted out. Just when I've become Paul's heroine. At least one boy likes me, even if it's a bed-wetting 8-year-old. It's because I encouraged him to send off a green crisp he found in a packet of Salt and Vinegar, with an 'it's not good enough' letter. Five packets came back by return of post—one given adoringly to me.

School meeting about Paris trip today—sounds great.

Drunken Louses

6

14th March

Only just got my diary back. There are some nice people in the world. I was sure someone had stolen it and accused everyone in sight. Pete, Mum and Daisy were the prime suspects because they're all so nosy. I really upset them—it's a wonder I've any friends left. Don't think they realized how unhappy it made me—not having it.

I hate losing things. Couldn't think of anything else at first. Was really angry, but then I began to forget about it and decided not to keep another diary. A parcel arrived for me today, couldn't understand it as it wasn't my birthday or anything. Don't know where it came from—no note or anything, just my diary. Hope someone had a good read—as long as they don't know me, that is!

Pete's been on at me to write the sex and contraception article for the school rag.

15th March

Paris tomorrow—mell idea. Got to be up by 5.30 a.m. and at
school by 6. Dad says he'll take me. My room's a complete tip.
Don't think anything I've got suits me. Mum's furious and says
I can't go till my room's tidy. No sympathy for the fact that
I'll look a complete Sharon—she even likes the way they look!

Pete's promised to look after Pinko while I'm away.

16th March

No Tunnel alas—trop cher, but it was fantastique in the bus.
Kate, Emma, John, Sheila and I all sat on the back seat and
shared our lunch. Wished Sheila had sat at the front as she
was threatening to throw up all the time. When we got to
France, we waved at all the Frenchmen in the cars behind.
Good response! Different from back home. Wish Sita had been
able to come too, but her parents wouldn't let her.

We stopped off for coffee on our way through Paris. Saw
the Eiffel Tower over grey rooftops. Went down the Champs-
Elysées past the Arc de Triomphe, over the Seine, which is full
of crap like the people who talk about cleaning the
environment and never do, but at least there were all these
beautiful barges with gardens on them, and children triking
round their decks. Wish I could live on one of them.

It's going to be a really good holiday. Coffee, cakes and wine all the time. Mr Rogers, our form teacher (who used to teach Pete 'the facts of life' and has been in the school for ever) is in charge. He refers to me as 'clever Pete Payne's little sister'—he's another creep but a nice one. He always runs the French trips. I think either he's having an affair with the French mistress, Miss Dunlop (who also comes), or he has a French mistress in Paris!

19th March

Chère Diary—je suis très fed up with this exchange business. J'arrived here three days ago and je ne peux comprend pas un mot of what anyone is saying to me. Totally fatiguée by the end of the day trying to understand and to parler la langue. Madame Cerveau is very gentille to me. Much better cook than Mum but she doesn't understand about moi not eating meat. She couldn't have understood my letter and I can't explain now. Madame looked très upset when I left her best roast veal and said 'No mad vache here', but I'm not going to eat any poor little calf that's been shut up in a wooden box all its life, and I'm definitely going to count snails and frogs' legs as meat! Had to give in over fish or they'd have been convinced I was mad—but I won't tell Pete.

I share a room with Marie—but she goes off and sees her friends without me. I know Madame tells her to stay with me—but she jamais does. Last night Madame allowed us to go out to a disco and Marie abandoned me. NO ONE asked MOI to dance except a real grease-gun midget with spots the size of saucers. Luckily Madame had insisted on us being back by 10 o'clock—she's very strict—so the agony was short. They all laughed and said I was a 'tapisserie'—I found out that meant 'wallflower'. I think I'm going to pleut.

20th March

Now I know why I'm so miserable—I'm on the blob again—a week early and I've forgotten to bring Tampax. Mum had warned me my period times might get upset by travelling. I've got terrible cramps and haven't even got the Mefenanic acid tablets the doctor gave me to use when they get bad. I'd been having time off school each month before I got them. Perhaps that explains my maths report! These tablets have made all the difference to the agonies—much better than aspirin and the other things I've tried.

Went for a 'promenade' to suss out a magasin that might sell Tampax. Didn't like to ask Madame or Marie. How could I? Only just arrived and immédiatement I'm asking for Tampax. Madame doesn't like me wandering around on my own. Wanted to send Marie's younger brother with me. No way.

At the local supermarché they were right up on the top shelf. Couldn't just sidle out with them. Had to ask twice in my best French, 'Avez-vous de Tampax si vous plaît?' Whole place—packed with old men—went silent. The shop assistant climbed up muttering, 'De Tampax, de Tampax, toujours de Tampax', pulled out the bottom one, and they all fell on his head along with a load of serviettes sanitaire. Quelle horreur! Très, très embarrassing.

23rd March

Madame took Marie and me to Paris yesterday by train. Sound—took hours through miles of French suburbia. Loved the metro, loved the Quai d'Orsay, loved the open-air markets, loved the Tuilleries where we sat eating baguette sandwiches and drinking coke (along with the other 200,000,000 daily coke drinkers around the world). Madame bought us une crêpe au chocolat for dessert. We passed a magasin called 'Preservatifs'. A whole shop devoted to condoms—every colour, flavour, shape and size. Pretended not to look while actually feasting. Madame and Marie showed no embarrassment. Je pense que les Françaises sont tres liberal. Used a pissoir outside the Pompidou Centre which played music while I peed. Five francs for a pee seems un peu cher. Un très exhausting day.

26th March

A letter from Pete! First one he's ever written. Not much of a letter though. Think Mum made him do it. All it was, was a scribbled note on the front of a 'Message to Young People'. Said 'Susie—I'm very worried about you—in France with all that wine—so I'm sending this leaflet to make sure you're not getting alcoholic. Hope you find it useful! Your loving and concerned brother—Pete'.

Personally, I would have liked him to have kept the leaflet for himself and sent me some juicy news about things like, 'How he and Brenda are getting on', 'Has Bovril had her kittens yet?', 'What Sam's up to', and 'Have Daisy and Paul gone yet?'.

How to tell when drinking is becoming a problem

- Do you drink because you have problems?
  To face up to stressful situations?
- Do you drink when you get mad at other people, your friends or parents?
- Do you often prefer to drink alone, rather than with others?
- Are you starting to get low marks? Are you skiving off work?
- Do you avoid being honest with others about your drinking?
- Do you ever get into trouble when you are drinking?
- Do you often get drunk when you drink, even when you do not mean to?
- Do you think you're big to be able to hold your drink?

Alcohol Consumption in Different Countries

Country	Consumption of litres of pure (100%) alcohol equivalent per year per person
France	12.7
Spain	10.8
Portugal	9.8
Italy	8.7
Australia	8.4
UK	7.6
USA	7.5
Japan	6.5

28th March

Although lots of time—there doesn't seem to be any privacy for writing. Even the toilets in other people's houses aren't the same sanctuary.

29th March

Un visite to EuroDisney par autobus avec mes amis—following the Mickey Mouse signs. When we arrived we joined the conveyor belt of wide-eyed kids and got transported to a squeaky-clean fantasy land.

For little kids, I dare say the place was great. They could feel like Cinderella, explore a jungle, become a spaceman, all within a couple of hours. However at our great age, I think although part of us wanted to believe, the other part was more than a bit cynical!

On the 'high street', we met a lady holding a bunch of balloons with a smile that was really sinister. She had spent two months in this 'Wild West' land and had not been outside the place. She whispered that she was constantly being watched by 'foxes' and she couldn't wait to get back to Birmingham where she lived. The 'foxes' she insisted were undercover employees who kept an eagle eye on the staff to ensure those enduring smiles were maintained. Just our luck, we thought, meeting a paranoic straight off. But then we came across 'Tigger' in the main square, who started to dance around with me, flirting and waving his willy-like tail. This was considered too frisky even for 'Tigger', and he was carted off by a couple of French gendarme characters with the order to 'get the hell back to Alice in Wonderland's tea party'.

Our behaviour overstepped the mark again at the car race track. John was a bit over the top in aggressive driving and was hauled out of his car for driving too fast and crossing the finishing line 'before your turn'. Had a bit of a feeling that 'big brother' Mickey was also watching from behind his plastic smile.

30th March

On our way home. Relief to be back with my friends again and to speak English for a change. Kate's family was upset she ate so little. John's family were all alcoholics. He was surprised they didn't have wine coming out of the taps, they drank so much. Mr Rogers was sitting on the seat in front, overhearing us. Breathing out heavily alcoholic and smoke-laden breath, he added that it wasn't just the French who had problems. In 1992, in the UK, the government spent £29,500,000,000 of our money on the National Health Service, and the same amount on education. And as individuals, we spent £10,000,000,000 on tobacco, £24,500,000,000 on alcohol, and £45,000,000,000 on food.

The government are total hypocrites, collecting £200 a second from alcohol taxes and only spending 0.1 pence per second on advertising its dangers. Really depressing. He said that alcohol drinking was involved in half of all murders, one in five of all child abuse cases, over half of all suicides, and a quarter of road traffic accidents where somebody is killed. I'm sure he knows the facts. He informed us that we didn't need to become alcoholics. With alcohol free wines, beers and ciders, we can still look 'hard' and drink at the same time.

Sheila laughed at my Tampax problems. She'd brought hers with her. She'd tried throwing her used ones into the lav, but they wouldn't flush away. She had to fish them out again, smuggle them through the house in a drippy paper bag, and throw them into the dustbin.

Saw an advert for using condoms as we were leaving Dover: 'Taking a condom on holiday with you won't save your life, using one might'. John said it was a bit late seeing it on the way home, and why were condoms called 'French letters'? Mr Rogers didn't know that, but said there was a legend that the sheath was invented by Dr Condom, doctor to King Charles II. But so much for legends, as he also knew (and I wonder how?) that randy Italians in the sixteenth century were using linen sheaths to stop themselves from getting syphilis. Quite funny really, seeing that everybody is now starting to use sheaths again to avoid getting that and other sexually transmitted diseases. Anyhow, Mr Rogers said that if they bothered to go on teaching Latin in schools nowadays we'd know that the word 'condom' actually comes from the Latin word 'condus' meaning 'a receptacle'. Just like having Pete around—getting all these facts ladled out to us. Thought I'd come on holiday to get away from all that.

There was a funny smell when we were unpacking the cases from the bus. One of the bottles of wine John was bringing back for his next party had broken. He couldn't believe that wine was so cheap in France. Think he's become addicted while living with his French family. They had two bottles of wine with every meal.

1st April
Slept all day yesterday—exhausted after journey back and by playing with Bov's new kittens (two alive, one dead—what's Pete been up to? Hope he hasn't been experimenting. I need to sort the bighead out.).

Got up knowing it was April Fools' Day but was fooled all the same. On way to newsagents greedy me saw a pound coin on the pavement outside John's house. Tried picking it up— burst of laughter from behind a hedge. He'd stuck it down with Super Glue. Total failure at catching Pete out. Even tried 'Brenda's on the phone' to get him out of bed, and he's much too clever for the salt in the sugar trick. Did catch Dad with my monster box of chocolates marked 'SUSIE'S CHOCOLATES—DO NOT TOUCH'. A great springing monster bonked him on the nose when he tried stealing one. Think he was more annoyed at getting caught out than anything else.

Pinko's got anorexia. Either that or she's been starved. Pete had done nothing! The cage was filthy and if she did get anything to eat, it was because Mum stuffed an occasional cabbage leaf in. Seem to have got fat in France. I was 62 kilos this morning.

Back to vegetarianism and no embarrassment. Mum knows my ways, and it's good not to have to eat 'veggies without the meat' all the time. It's not that I'm totally committed—like vegans, who don't even eat milk, eggs or cheese. Vegetarianism makes sense to me. You can get all you need to survive if you make sure you have all the proteins and vitamins—and Mum's outstanding on reading the labels. Pete used to think it mad to eat lentils, cheese and beans to get protein when you can have steak: now he's not so sure with mad cow disease.

4th April

At last, with her huge experience—ha ha, Louise has started to write her guide to boys . . .

My Guide To **Boys**

by Louise Heathers

BOYS . . . BOYS . . . BOYS . . . BOYS . . . BOYS . . . BOYS—or why I hate them. When I most want them to notice me they don't. I spend hours getting done up and they don't even notice. I suppose it might bring a bit of excitement into some girls' lives but I just find it obnoxious. When I'm insulted and sulk and I'm waiting for them to apologize they don't, 'cos they think it's not macho to say sorry.

Occasionally I have these fantasies about the boy of my dreams arriving on my doorstep with a huge bunch of flowers, ready to whisk me away on a huge red motorbike. Some chance!!!

I try to pretend not to be the slightest bit interested. This actually is an awful lot harder than it sounds. When someone I fancy saunters over to borrow my homework, how am I supposed to say 'No' in a calm collected voice when my stomach is raving and my knees are jelly?

Then all I get for my pains is that they go off with my best friend. Boys like that just aren't worth the bother.

This certainly isn't the way I feel about boys. She's even more desperate than I am.

6th April

No boy with a nose would come within a mile of me at the moment as I stink of anti-louse stuff. Paul's leaving present to the family when he, Daisy and Aunty Jo finally left was nits. Aunty Jo admitted it to Mum in one of their endless phone calls. I had thought it was just dandruff when I felt itchy in France. Hope my nits enjoyed their French holiday. Mum found the little beasties.

Dad—the beastie exterminator—was in his element. He said that in a recent survey asking mums whether their children had had head lice in the previous year, one in three said 'Yes'. But worse was to come. If our heads were looked at by a 'beastie hunting' expert, they were FIVE times more likely to find them than our mums. On average, the beasties have been feeding away on our heads for four months before we know we've got them.

Dad was even willing to give us the facts about the louse's sex life. The life of a louse is a mere three weeks. They like everybody's hair but some more than others. They prefer short hair to long, clean hair to dirty (no, that's not a mistake). They seem to spread only directly by head to head contact, they cannot jump, hop, fly or swim, and they can spend time on several heads a day.

What the head louse does when it gets on to your head— between the hairs—is to take a good bite at your skin (up to 200 bites a day per louse). When it bites, its spit irritates your skin and makes you want to scratch. Having bitten and sucked out a little bit of your blood, it then shits. When you scratch, you rub their shit into the bites and the irritation gets worse. The next thing they do (at seven days of age) is start having sex (which I haven't managed yet, though I think Charlotte has) and laying eggs, which they attach to the roots of your hair. A short, but not such a lousy life after all.

To stop this grossness you first have to find the beast, which is the hard part. Mum needed her glasses to find them as they are nearly transparent and a bit smaller than the head of a match; and the eggs on the hair are pinhead-sized and flesh-coloured. Dad was really mean and cruel. He said that regular combing breaks the legs off the lice. Life is not so easy for a legless louse and they fall off our heads and die. (If animals can feel pain, then why can't lice? What about Lice Rights?)

Mum made the whole family use the smelly anti-louse lotion. Luckily—if used properly—it not only kills the lice but protects you for a bit against getting them again. We had to leave it on over night and couldn't go swimming for two days after we'd used it or blow-dry our hair (chlorine in water and heat stop it working).

EASTER HOLIDAYS begin today—so don't have to stink out the school.

7th April
Going to have a spending spree. Blow all my saved money. Phoned up Mary to come too. She said she'd love to—amazed she's actually leaving her boyf's side to grace me with her presence.

8th April
Caught up on some gossip with Mary yesterday and had a laugh trying on outrageous outfits in Miss Selfridge's. So annoying, unless you're thin and leggy, none of the clothes fit or look good. Mary thinks it's stupid to diet and we're all right as we are. She may be—but I feel less certain for myself.

Still, why should we try to be like the models in the adverts? They're all touched up and specially photographed to look thinner than they really are, anyway.

I think all those French painters we saw had it right—no clothes and none of that thin nonsense. Pete says that boys don't really like thin girls, and that it's their minds and personalities which matter. Don't believe a word of it. Mary saw him at the cinema without his glasses and with his hand down the top of 'all-breasts' Brenda's blouse. She says the air was heavy with testosterone. I suggested to Pete that *his* mind was on Brenda's *body* especially as she doesn't have any personality. He shouted at me to mind my own f.......g business. Don't know where he learns this kind of language.

7 **Glands**, Fevers and **Revision**

10th April

Feel awful—hate myself—especially the bit called my throat which is really sore. My tonsils are like two mountains with someone gouging the tops off with blunt knives. If I survive this I promise never to think those thoughts about Sam again.

No sympathy from Mum, needless to say. She never believes any of us since she found Sally shopping half an hour after she'd claimed she was at death's door with tonsillitis. Pete just did his 'I am the world's number one budding medic' act—told me to shut up and take an aspirin. Bloody know all. He's only got to get a headache and he thinks he's dying.

What a waste of holiday.

11th April

Worse—Sam where are you? Actually anyone who would be nice to me would do.

12th April

Worse, worser, worstest. Pete still doesn't believe I am really ill. He won't come close to me though. Don't want him to, but still wish Sam would.

13th April

Worstest of all. It's supposed to be Good Friday, but it's Friday the thirteenth and ghastly. Mum rang the doctor who said most sore throats are due to viruses or bacteria but you usually can't tell which so just to give me paracetamol or aspirin. Big deal. Aspirin for this, aspirin for that. Nowadays, it's even aspirin for heart attacks. Thousands of years of medical science and that's all they come up with?

Sam called to see Pete today—didn't even come up to see me. I hate him, I hate Pete, I hate the world. I'm going to stay in bed and starve for ever and ever, and then they'll all be sorry.

14th April

Dragged down to the doctor's. Much the illest person in the waiting room. The doctor was OK but didn't seem very interested. She made things worse by poking the back of my throat with a stick. Said she'd send it off to see what grows. Yugh—monsters with claws probably.

She then sent me to the nurse who took all my blood. I asked her if she had had a starring part in *Interview With the Vampire*. I turned pale and droopy at the end of the needle.

15th April

Dad did his usual Easter egg hunt. Strange, but I still enjoy these rituals, raw tonsils or not. So does Pete, who stole all my eggs and ate them, saying I was too fat already. Tried to get my own back by saying I'd tell Mum about him and Brenda. She's someone Mum wouldn't approve of. He said he wished there was something to tell!

Not much fun having Easter and feeling so awful.

20th April

The nurse from the doctor's rang up yesterday to say, 'She's got glandular fever.' So I am ill, even if no one else believed me. Funny thing is, I don't feel so bad now—just floppy and exhausted, like a wet rag.

Pete's been making kissing noises at me since he read the 'Glandular Fever' leaflet the nurse gave Mum. (But I haven't kissed properly since Christmas. It was John, who smells awful and tried to touch my breasts. Maybe it was him that did this. Perhaps Kate'll get it too.)

Glandular Fever

(1) WHAT CAUSES IT?

A virus called the Epstein Barr virus (after the men who discovered it).

(2) IS IT CATCHING?

Yes—it is an infectious disease and is spread from one person to another. However it's not very infectious and usually you have to be in close contact with a person who has it in order to catch it. That's why it's sometimes called the 'kissing disease', but kissing isn't the only way of getting it. It can also be spread from one person to another like a cold—by breathing in the virus or swallowing it.

(3) WHO GETS IT?

It is very common, and about one in ten children aged 14 and 15 have had it, often without knowing. By the age of 18, over half of young people will have had it. Boys and girls get it about equally, and adults can get it too.

(4) HOW DO YOU KNOW THAT YOU HAVE GOT IT?

You nearly always get a sore throat and swollen glands in your neck. If it's glandular fever, these do not get better as quickly as sore throats and swollen glands normally do. Other glands may also swell up in your groin or under your arms. Sometimes you even get a rash. You'll usually feel tired, unwell, and will have a headache and a fever.

(5) HOW CAN YOU PROVE THAT YOU HAVE GOT IT?

You have to see your doctor, who can do a blood test. This will usually show whether or not you have glandular fever (or whether you have had it in the past). There are also other viruses which can make you feel unwell in the same way.

(6) HOW LONG WILL IT LAST?

This varies. Some young people get it and then get better so quickly that they do not even realize they have had it. For most, it lasts about three weeks.

First week—very sore throat, swollen glands, temperature; you will feel very unwell and like staying in bed.

Second week—fever going down, and you will feel a bit better.

Third week—you will feel much better; fever has gone, but you will still feel very tired, even when doing very little.

(7) CAN IT LAST FOR YEARS?

Normally you get better in a few weeks, but you may still get tired very easily for some further weeks, or months, afterwards. For a few people the effects last even longer.

(8) IS THERE ANY TREATMENT?

None at the moment—though you may be given an antibiotic by your doctor when you first have a sore throat, before it is realized that you are suffering from glandular fever. This won't do you any harm, but neither will it help cure the glandular fever because antibiotics don't kill viruses (only bacteria). The only treatment is to take paracetamol regularly (always check the instructions on the bottle or packet to see how much, and how often to take it). This will help bring your fever down, help relieve the pain in your throat, and will generally make you feel a bit better.

(9) SHOULD YOU STAY IN BED AND REST A LOT?

Whether you stay in bed or not depends entirely on how you feel. For the first week or two most people do feel like staying in bed, resting, sleeping, and having drinks and food that is easy to swallow—jellies, soups, ice-creams. Later on you may still feel like resting and sleeping more than usual. Your body, under these circumstances, is usually very good at telling you how much you can do.

(10) WHAT ABOUT PLAYING SPORTS?

It is not a good idea to do sports in the first three weeks of the illness, and you probably won't feel like it. You may even get very tired after mild exercise for weeks or months, so be guided by how you feel.

(11) WILL IT AFFECT YOUR WORK?

During the first weeks of the illness most people find it very difficult to work and concentrate. When you get back to school, it's best to tell your teachers what's been the matter and they should be sympathetic. Show them this leaflet if they aren't! Most children find work a problem for some weeks after the illness because of tiredness, depression and lethargy, but it does get better and everyone recovers.

(12) IS GLANDULAR FEVER THE SAME AS CHRONIC FATIGUE SYNDROME?

No. Chronic fatigue syndrome is also known as ME or myalgic encephalitis. Other names include 'Yuppie 'flu' and 'Post viral syndrome'.

What people complain of is: aching in the muscles after exercise, excessive tiredness, poor concentration, memory loss and depression. There has been a lot of discussion about whether this really exists as an actual disease. Nobody has managed to find out what causes it. We do know that a small number of people who have glandular fever, 'flu, or some other viral nasty, can go on to get these sorts of problems, which may last for months. Fortunately they are rare.

Sometimes these things occur out of the blue. There is no specific test you can do to tell whether or not you have chronic fatigue syndrome. It usually gets better by itself.

24th April

Kate told me I'd missed a timed essay for GCSE English—will I fail? Made Mum give Pete a note for school. The teachers always think you're just skiving even if you're dying. Bet Pete forgets.

2nd May

Mum spoke to my teacher. Hate her doing that but it seems I haven't missed out on my GCSE. My teacher said that if I had missed an essay, all they would do is take the best of one of the ones I have already done. If it had been worse, and I had missed more, it would've been OK to get a note from my doctor.

Horrible fright today—thought Bovril had broken her leg. She was limping around trying to keep up with her kittens. She's only just back from being 'done' at the vets'. I found this huge great bump and something sticking out of it. She mewed pathetically every time I touched it. I panicked and rang Mum at work. She came home at lunch-time and said it looked like a bee sting. Then I remembered that Bov had been playing around with a bee—trust her to pick the first bee of the year. We removed the sting very carefully and then Mum said to leave Bov alone, as she would get better by herself.

She also said that if it had been me that had been stung, I should have put some bicarbonate of soda (mixed with water) on the swelling, and that if it had been a wasp, some vinegar. Said it is easy to remember which is which because it's 'Bee for bicarbonate and Winegar for wasp'. I said it's a good job it isn't the other way around!

Apparently people sometimes have a very bad reaction to a sting. They get massive swelling around it, which can spread. If this happens (it is quite rare), they need a doctor—quickly.

Dead bored being at home, dead tired if I try doing anything else. Searched Pete's room—found this book of jokes in his wardrobe (along with three old copies of *Playboy* and a couple of other wank mags). Light relief at last, so cheered up.

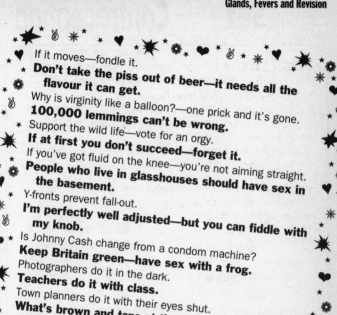

If it moves—fondle it.

Don't take the piss out of beer—it needs all the flavour it can get.

Why is virginity like a balloon?—one prick and it's gone.

100,000 lemmings can't be wrong.

Support the wild life—vote for an orgy.

If at first you don't succeed—forget it.

If you've got fluid on the knee—you're not aiming straight.

People who live in glasshouses should have sex in the basement.

Y-fronts prevent fall-out.

I'm perfectly well adjusted—but you can fiddle with my knob.

Is Johnny Cash change from a condom machine?

Keep Britain green—have sex with a frog.

Photographers do it in the dark.

Teachers do it with class.

Town planners do it with their eyes shut.

What's brown and taps at the window?—a baby in a microwave.

Definition of a man—the redundant end of a penis.

Rugby players do it with odd-shaped balls.

Adam came first, men always do.

Careful—more than two shakes is masturbation.

Keep pop music alive—kill the producer of Top of the Pops.

6th May

Pete's nagging me about the article on sex and contraception. Thinks I've got nothing better to do, just because I'm ill. He's revising away for his 'A's. I should be revising for GCSE, but I can't concentrate. Pete gave me a pile of contraception leaflets, to copy out the best bits. Must be anonymous though—can't have the whole school thinking *I* know anything about it.

You, **Sex** and **Contraception**

> **What I think is**: first—you don't have to have sex. This book, *Sexual Behaviours in Great Britain*, says that 80% of girls and 70% of boys haven't had sexual intercourse yet (OK, they have done other things together), so you don't actually have to have intercourse to be part of the 'in' crowd.
> Whether you have had sex or not, you need to know about sex and contraception.

How good is your knowledge about contraception?
Test yourself on the following 16 easy questions.
(Answers on page 65.)

1. Do you need to have intercourse to get pregnant?
2. Can the woman get pregnant if she doesn't have an orgasm?
3. Can you get pregnant if you don't both 'come' together?
4. Is withdrawal a safe method?
5. How long after making love does 'emergency' contraception work?
6. Can the first bit of cum make her pregnant?
7. Can you rely on the 'safe period'?
8. During which days of her period is it 'safe' to make love without contraception?
9. Is the contraceptive sponge a very reliable method?
10. Does the 'pill' help protect you against sexually transmitted diseases including AIDS?
11. Is it OK to use spermicides alone?
12. Are IUDs (coils) a good method of contraception for teenagers?
13. Do condoms help stop you from getting sexually transmitted diseases?
14. Can you only have sex by having intercourse?
15. Does the 'pill' make you fat?
16. How long do sperm survive in the vagina?

Answers

1. ✖ No —if some of the man's sperm get near the entrance to the woman's vagina, they can swim up it, though this is very unlikely to happen!
2. ✔ Yes—female orgasm doesn't, as far as we know, influence whether a woman gets pregnant or not.
3. ✔ Yes—neither partner has to 'come' for pregnancy to occur, as the man can leak sperm before he ejaculates.
4. ✖ No—often the man doesn't pull out in time, and he may leak some sperm before he does. Remember that just one drop of semen contains enough sperm to populate the whole of New Zealand. Even so, it is better to pull out than not!
5. It is effective if taken up to seventy-two hours after making love (NOT after missing the last period—please note).
6. ✔ Yes—before a man ejaculates, he leaks a bit of semen which may act as a lubricant, but may also contain sperm.
7. ✖ No—the 'safe period' is not a very reliable method. It needs to be taught and you need to be able to chart your periods, your temperature, and your vaginal mucus.
8. None are 100% safe—but some days are worse than others. If you have a regular 28-day cycle, then days seven to fifteen after the beginning of your period are the worst days.
9. ✖ No—it has a 25% failure rate, but it is certainly better than nothing.
10. ✖ No—this is the method least likely to protect you against sexually transmitted diseases (even though it's a reliable way not to get pregnant—if you remember to take it, that is!)
11. ✖ No—it's not safe to use spermicides alone, but again, if they're the only thing you've got around, they're better than nothing and do help to protect against AIDS.
12. ✖ No—they are not recommended unless you've already had a baby. IUDs can lead to an infection of your tubes and make you infertile.
13. ✔ Yes—this is absolutely true and is one of their huge advantages.
14. ✖ No—one of the best forms of contraception is all the lovely sexy things you can do and have orgasm without actually having intercourse itself.

15. Not taking the pill may make you fatter—if you get pregnant! A small percentage of women may get fatter on the pill, but you can almost always find one that suits you.

16. The average ones among the whole 300 million of them in each ejaculate survive for four days, but remember there is a lunatic fringe which may survive for six to seven days. (The egg is more fragile. There is only one, and unless it becomes fertilized, it dies within twelve to twenty-four hours.)

If you didn't score well on this
you certainly shouldn't be scoring at all!

Contraception

From what I've found out, there's no ideal method of contraception. They've all got their pros and cons. What's certain is that you're *very likely* to get pregnant/get someone pregnant if you decide to take a chance.

How likely are you to get pregnant without contraception ?

● If you have sex when an egg has been released (about fourteen days before a period), there's a 30% risk of getting pregnant. (This may not sound all that risky, but would you cross the road if there was a 1 in 3 chance of getting killed?)

● If you have sex somewhere around the middle of the cycle (when the egg is normally released), there is still a 20% risk of getting pregnant.

● At other times, the risk can still be as high as 10%. Most people don't know when they ovulate and although the egg doesn't hang about waiting to get fertilized (a mere twelve to twenty-four hours), the sperm hang around for several days. So even if the egg isn't released until a few days after having unprotected sexual intercourse, there may still be some hungry sperm waiting.

How do you choose which contraceptive

The important thing is to find out all about the different methods available, and then you and your boyfriend/girlfriend can decide which method is best for your relationship and go for it. You both need to feel 'happy' and safe with the method you are using. What's right for one couple is not necessarily right for another. If, after a while, you decide you don't like what you're using, you can always change your mind and try something different.

What can happen . . .

She thought it was wrong to have sex before marriage. One night her parents were out and one thing led to another. He respected her views, but they both lost control. He meant to withdraw, **but he didn't**. He thought she should have been on the pill, **but she wasn't**. She thought he should have used a condom, **but he didn't**. She should have gone for emergency contraception, **but she didn't**. They should have talked about it, **but they couldn't**. She thought she was going to have a baby, **but she wasn't**. They shouldn't have been so lucky, **but they were**.

In one study, 70% of couples had had unprotected sex the first time. You may get away with it once, *but don't count on it.*

The choice

You can choose between condoms, the female condom, the combined pill, the progesterone-only pill, an IUD (coil), a diaphragm (cap), spermicides, the 'safe' period, the contraceptive sponge or withdrawal. It sounds like a lot of choice, but it's less than it seems, as many of the methods aren't very effective.

Where to get it

You can go to your general practitioner, or any GP. Other places are family planning clinics, or a Brook Advisory Clinic if there is one near you. The pill is free from your GP and from clinics. Condoms are free from clinics, and some GPs give them out free.

How condoms work

A condom is a sheath of thin rubber which is rolled over the erect penis and stops the sperm getting into the womb.

Why I like condoms

- 'They're easy to get hold of from chemists, garages, pubs'
- 'They protect me against sexually transmitted diseases'
- 'They help protect me against AIDS'
- 'He has to pay for them'
- 'She has to pay for them'
- 'I don't have to take chemicals all the time'
- 'It's less messy afterwards'
- 'They're easy to carry around and make me feel that there might just be a chance!'
- 'They are very safe and well tested'
- 'I can get her to put it on me so that she knows we're safe'

Why I don't like condoms

- 'It cuts down on the sensation'
- 'You can't trust a man to use one properly'
- 'I worry all the time that it's going to slip off'
- 'It's like making love with a ski glove on'
- 'It's a passion killer'
- 'He'll think I'm cheap if I carry a condom'
- 'It's like tying the knot and throwing it away makes me feel I'm getting rid of the whole population of America all at one time'

Summary

Condoms are very effective — **98%** reliable.

You can buy them everywhere (well, almost everywhere).

They protect you from sexually transmitted diseases, and they don't harm your body in any way.

The Female Condom

The female condom is also known as the 'Femidom'. It's very good at stopping you getting pregnant and preventing you getting sexually transmitted diseases. What's more, the woman has control over it as she puts it into her vagina (though the rim gets left outside) and one size fits all women and all penises! Some family planning clinics provide them free, but usually you have to buy them and they are a bit pricey at around a pound each.

The Pill

How it works
It contains two hormones—oestrogen and progesterone—which stop the woman's egg being released each month.

Why I like the pill
+ 'It's the safest method I know'
+ 'I find it doesn't interfere, when we want to make love, as we don't have to stop and fiddle around'
+ '... really easy, I only have to remember to take the pill every day and it's done'
+ 'After all, they're free from GPs or family planning clinics, and that's what makes the difference for me'
+ '... makes my periods not so heavy and always on time, which I like, as it helps knowing when they're going to come'
+ '... don't have to worry, it's all her responsibility'
+ 'For me, I like being in control of my own body, after all, if something happens, it's me that gets pregnant'
+ 'It's so bloody convenient'

Why I don't like the pill
- 'It doesn't protect me against AIDS, or other sexually transmitted diseases'

- 'I keep forgetting to take it, and then I have to use condoms for a week anyway'
- 'I don't like the idea of filling my body up with hormones'
- 'My friend put on weight and had headaches when she was on the pill and I don't want that'
- 'I don't think it's right her having to take those hormone things all the time. Must have some effects, mustn't it?'
- '. . . I worry about the side-effects'

Summary: **The pill is the best contraception**

for not getting pregnant, as long as you remember to take it, but it's not so good if you want to avoid AIDS and other sexually transmitted diseases. One option, of course, is to use both. There are some side-effects from the pill, but most women feel fine and don't have any problems.

Minor side-effects These might not sound minor to you, or feel minor when you're suffering from them, but most of them pass off or settle down if you change to a different pill.
- depression
- headaches
- going off sex (the most efficient contraceptive!)
- feeling sick
- tender breasts
- moodiness

Most women feel absolutely fine on the pill.

The pill and cancer There have been a lot of scares about this in the last few years. The pill will protect you from cancer of the ovary and cancer of the womb, which is good. Long-term use of the pill (more than five years) when you're young results in a slightly increased risk of getting breast and cervical cancer (though not all the studies agree on this).

Smoking and the pill These don't go together as you are more likely to get some of the serious side-effects if you smoke.

The pill and blood clots There is a slightly increased risk of blood clots with the pill, especially if you smoke.

Possible problems

The Cap

How it works
It is a piece of soft rubber which the woman puts into her vagina to cover her cervix (the entrance to her womb) and stop the sperm meeting the egg.

Why I like the cap

+ 'I thought it would be really difficult, but it was just like putting in a tampon'

+ '. . . I like the cap better than the pill. I got fed-up having to take the pill every day. I don't like the idea of taking hormones all the time. They might do something to my body'

+ 'The great thing about using it is you don't have to stop and fiddle about in the middle, like with a condom. I put it in before I know we're going to make love'

+ '. . . means I'm in charge'

Why I don't like the cap

– 'It all sounds really messy to me, and I don't like the idea of putting something inside me'

– 'It's a real bother as it needs to be fitted by a doctor, so you can't just buy it over the counter'

– '. . . not safe enough for me'

<u>**Summary:**</u> The cap is a good method if you are really motivated and don't mind putting things in and out of yourself.

It's **96%** effective, though young people seem to have a slightly higher failure rate — perhaps they don't always put it in, or check that it's in the right place, or use enough spermicide with it.

The cap gives you a bit of protection against sexually transmitted diseases, **but not as much as a condom.**

Unreliable but widely used methods

The 'natural' or 'rhythm' method

The idea behind this is to find out when you ovulate (about fourteen days before the next period) by a combination of taking your temperature, noting changes in the vaginal mucus, and charting the dates of your periods. It's good in that you get to know the changes occurring in your body, and there are no side-effects (other than pregnancy!). But it's a very unreliable method unless you have regular periods, have been well taught, and are very careful — as sex is limited to 'safe' days, rather than when you feel like it.

'Withdrawal'

This is when the man takes his penis out of the woman's vagina just before he ejaculates. The trouble is ***it's not very effective*** — but if you're going to have sex, it's certainly better than nothing. Much, ***much*** safer is to use one of the other methods.

Emergency contraception

A lot of people don't know or do anything about emergency contraception. They just behave like ostriches, dig their head in, and hope it will be OK. In a recent study of women wanting abortions, 70% had known they were at risk of getting pregnant (no contraception or a split condom). If everyone at risk used emergency contraception, at least 100,000 abortions in the UK alone could be avoided.

There are two types of emergency contraception: pill or coil.

Pill

These are sometimes called the 'morning after pill', but that term is totally wrong. In fact, you have up to *three days (seventy-two hours)* in which to get hold of the pills. It's best to take them sooner rather than later — though there's no need to wake a doctor up in the middle of the night!

You get the pills from any doctor, family planning clinic, or accident and emergency department of a hospital. You can't buy them over the counter. If there's any chance that you've taken a chance, make sure you get emergency advice. It's much better than needing an abortion or having an unwanted pregnancy. The pills can make you feel sick, but if they do, there are some other tablets you can take which help.

This is not a method to use regularly, *only in emergencies*. And if emergencies are happening once a week, it's time you sorted yourself out, as you are only kidding yourself that you are not having sex.

It's very good at stopping you getting pregnant (98% effective), but it's no good at stopping you from getting sexually transmitted diseases. All you have to do is take two lots of pills with a twelve-hour interval.

Coil or IUD

Very few people know that if you have a coil put in *up to five days* after unprotected intercourse it can work as emergency contraception and prevent you from getting pregnant.

It is probably best to opt for emergency contraceptive pills, but if it is *more than 72 hours* after the event, and you've not done anything about it, go to a GP or family planning clinic as quickly as possible and get a coil put in. It can be taken out after your next period or left in if you want to continue with it as a form of contraception.

So don't forget to get emergency contraception if you forget to use something in the first place.

That's it—good luck!

14th May

I was in a total state this morning—couldn't decide WHAT to wear. Went through three changes of clothing. As soon as I think I look slightly OK I decide it's not good enough and I change again.

I'm back at school with GCSE exams in three weeks. Massive catch-up needed. If I fail my exams I'm not sure what I'll do. I'll probably blame myself for being a lazy cow for the last two years—though it wasn't my fault I was ill.

I'll be a complete failure—a nothing. It's a terrible pressure, all these exams, especially as I don't know what I'd say to my friends if they asked me how I'd done and I'd failed. Mum says I can only do my best, but whatever she says I know she'll be sad if I don't do well. (Not even sure that Dad knows I'm taking them.)

I wish I could turn the clock back and begin my revision over. I've got Mrs Smith's revision plan to work to again. I'll really do what she says this time, unlike for mocks.

REVISION PLAN

1 Estimate the total number of working hours you have till the exams. (I've got 14 weekdays with 3 hours to revise after school, plus 3 weekends with 5 hours for revising each day, which makes a total of 14 x 3 + 6 x 5 which = 72 hours.)

2 Give equal time to each subject. (I've got 8 to do, so that gives me exactly 9 hours revision for each.)

3 At this stage, there is no way you can revise everything on every subject. Therefore decide—for each subject—what you know least about, and get that sorted first. If you have any time over—then, and only then, go over the stuff you know best. (Told Mum that as I know nothing best, and don't have time to revise everything, this is going to be tough. Nice Mum started asking me questions about history—all of which I could answer!)

4 Only work for a maximum of an hour at a time and then have a break. After one hour your brain doesn't concentrate so well. (Not sure whether my brain ever gets going—wish I was more like Pete.)

5 Remember it's relatively easy to get half marks for each question. It is many, many times more difficult to get really high marks. It is therefore better to answer all the questions reasonably well than to answer half the questions really well.

18th May

I'm always late for everything. And I'm an optimist and think I can do much more than I actually can, but my revision is going well. There's no time to write my diary, but I'm feeling less tired, thank goodness.

Mum's in a state about Brenda. She thinks she's a bad influence on Pete. She smokes and goes to pubs, and Mum's sure she's on drugs. (I know she is, and so does Pete!)

Bov's in a state about her kittens being given away. It's better than drowning them, but she doesn't understand that.

8 Exams and *Abuse*

4th June

Panic, panic, panic. I can't sleep, I can't stop eating, I can't concentrate. I'm tired all the time, I've forgotten everything I've ever learnt, I'm terrified of everything going blank when I see the exam paper. I can't do any revision as it all disappears again.

Being at school's worse—mass hysteria—everybody scared shitless! I think the staff are really pissed off. Mr MacIntosh—the head—did one of his 'now then children, don't panic' speeches. Quite scary, with his wire specs, white hair and crinkled face. He looks about seven feet tall up on stage.

It may be too late to revise now. Most of you will experience panic at one time or another when faced with that dreaded moment when you are first given the examination paper. Some of the things which will happen when you read it are good. More adrenalin will be pumped round your body, your heart will beat faster, and you will become generally more alert. However, some of your reactions may be less positive—being unable to concentrate, thinking your mind has gone blank, feeling sure that you know nothing.

So wouldn't it be good if there were a few very simple tricks to help you cope with the bad aspects of panic? Well, there are. They are things that have been learnt by people who have taken many, many examinations. They can help a great deal, but they need a bit of practising.

What really STOPS THE PANIC is if, instead of rushing in and being convinced you will never finish the exam paper in time, you spend a few minutes getting yourself organized before you start writing. Many marks may be gained as a result of those few minutes planning.

So:

First—and foremost if you feel yourself panicking when you get the exam paper—count slowly to ten before reading it. This will only take ten seconds but will allow your nerves just that tiny bit of time to calm down.

Second—read the instructions carefully as to HOW MANY questions you have to answer. (You will not get one single extra mark for answering more questions than you need to.)

Third—read the instructions again and find out how much time you have for the examination as a whole. Then divide the number of questions you have to answer into the total time, and work out how long you can spend on each question. (5 questions in the 86 minutes left in a 90-minute exam—after the 4 minutes that it has taken you to do the things listed here—means about 17 minutes for each answer.) Spend ONLY that amount of time on each answer.

Fourth—read each question carefully, decide which you want to answer, and quickly write down notes on everything you know about each one BEFORE you start to write the full answer on the one you know best. The reasons for this are very simple:

   a) If each question is marked out of the SAME amount—say 20—to get 12 out of 20 is fairly straightforward; to get 14 out of

20 you have to be very good; to get 17 or more out of 20 you would have to know the topic inside out.

b) If you spend half the total exam time answering the question you know best really well, and then only manage two more answers of the five you should have done, then you might get 41 marks (17 for your excellent one and 12 for each of the others). But if you do all five just fairly well (12 marks each) you will get 60—simple really.

Writing short notes at the beginning—on every question you are going to answer while your mind is still fresh—prevents you from panicking about not having anything to say on the ones you know least about.

He ended by wishing us 'All the very best of luck'—nice but a bit pompous. It's easy for him to say that—he doesn't have to do the exams.

Pete's into A levels. We're not allowed to talk about his exams. We get screamed at if we ask how they went. Don't know what he's making such a fuss about—he's bound to do well.

Dad and Mum totally fed up today. They're thinking of going to live somewhere else till it's all over.

5th June

Exams start tomorrow. Resolutions:

I won't panic

I will read the questions

I will look and see how much time I have

I will see how many questions I have to answer

I will write short notes first

I will do my best handwriting

I will have all my pens and pencils and my calculator with me.

HELP!

P.S. I must remember to take my hayfever spray regularly.

6th June

The English exam was easy but I messed it up. Didn't see the question on the last page. So much for my resolutions. I had tummy pains all the way through. Curse periods. I think examiners should make allowances.

It really made a difference—Mum and Dad being so relaxed with me about the exams. Kate's mum hassles her every time she wants to go out. Even on a Friday night she goes on about 'but what about your homework? Have you thought about the revision you need to do for the exams?' Right in front of her friends. It's really not on—would make me want to do just the opposite.

What do parents think? That we want to fail **our exams**? At least Mum and Dad seem to trust me (most of the time anyway). They remind me to have rests from work, and they bring me cups of coffee. Mum makes a special effort to have meals on time and to give me treats, but today Dad's hardly speaking to me. He spent half the evening picking the phone up downstairs and finding I was still talking to Kate. All we were doing was complaining to one another about how immature and weedy all the boys in our year are—there's not one that's fanciable.

8th June

Maths OK. But Sheila wasn't. She walked out sobbing—half-way through. Everybody looked at her as she went. Nobody could understand. She's the brain.

9th June

Thank God for weekends. Kept to my timetable of revision. One hour biology, cup of tea, one hour history, cup of tea and a walk. All was well till I looked at an old GCSE history paper and couldn't answer two of the five questions. I'll never manage.

Rang Kate and Emma to come for lunch. Kate said she couldn't make it for lunch, but came afterwards. I don't think she likes eating. It turns out the reason Sheila walked out yesterday was nothing to do with maths!

She'd been depressed for ages because a man had tried to rape her. It all started a year ago when she got a job working part-time in a café belonging to a friend of her dad. It was OK for the first few months, but then the owner insisted on walking her home, even though she lived very near. During the Christmas holidays, every time he walked her home he tried to make her hold his hand. She didn't like it but thought he'd had too much to drink or something. She started to dread going there, but didn't want to give it up because of the money.

One night towards the end of January he was walking her home and holding her hand. Then, still holding her hand, he put her hand in his pocket. She suddenly realized that there was a hole in his pocket, because her hand was touching something warm and hard. She tried pulling her hand away. They were still walking towards her house and she couldn't say anything. When they finally got there he let go and she ran in crying.

She felt she couldn't tell her mum who wanted to know what was wrong. Sheila said that she was just tired, and went up to bed and cried herself to sleep. She didn't think she would hear from him again, but the next week, while she was out, he phoned and her mum said she could work that night. She knew Sheila needed the money.

Sheila felt incredibly scared and she was right. On the way home, although she'd told him she didn't want him anywhere near her, he tried to grab her and push her down an alley, in spite of the fact that there were other people around. Sheila said he was foul and smelt disgusting, but what was most scary was how strong he was. However, Sheila kept her head and her cool, perhaps because she had been expecting this to happen, and screamed very loudly. The guy swore at her and pushed off.

Sheila couldn't tell anyone, because she felt partly responsible, but she thought about it all the time. She hated that man and wanted to kill him. Since then she has stopped working, but she sits and goes through it again and again, thinking about what she should have done. It hurt her to think about it—really hurt she said. It made her feel so ashamed and humiliated. Once, when it all got particularly bad, she couldn't even kiss her father. She knew that if she did she'd be sick. Sometimes she blamed her mother and her best friend for not noticing that she was unhappy. She'd hinted but they'd never caught on. The exams were the last straw—but at least now her parents know.

Luckily I was able to tell my mum about the flasher who pulled out his shrivelled willy in the cathedral when we were on holiday in France. Mat and Pete thought it was funny—but it wasn't for me. Mum's great. She said nothing happens in life that is so bad that you can't tell someone about it.

11th June

History today—managed all five questions—hurrah! All that revision was worth while. French in the afternoon—un complet disastre, et je suis miserable maintenant.

Pete thinks that men like Sheila's boss should have their balls cut off. Mum says you can't do that, they need some kind of help. Still the same message from her. Everyone (including Pete) should know when to say NO—like my friend Jane did when we were 13 and it happened to her.

The only time it nearly happened to me was when some girlfriends and I were coming home across the park after a party. Some older boys followed us home, calling us 'slags'. I've never been so scared. I thought they were going to rape us, especially as another girl, who was a bit drunk, was leading them on. Luckily, they went away after about fifteen minutes. Since then I've tried to follow Sal's tips on being careful:

* If possible I stick to well-lit and well-used routes when going to and from school and people's houses.
* I always try to walk with someone I know.
* I never hitch-hike although sometimes I would like to.
* I never play in or hang around in lifts or toilets (too smelly anyhow).
* I only carry the money I need (if I have any!) and don't advertise it in public.
* I try to tell Mum and Dad where I'm going and what time I'll be home (they always ask anyhow).
* If I go to a party, I make sure I know beforehand how I'm going to get home.
* If anyone tried to touch me in a way I didn't like, I'd say NO loudly and firmly, and tell someone about it.
* If I was attacked, I'd scream and run to where there were other people (better to run than to face the attacker).
* If I couldn't run, I'd scream and kick, or knee the attacker in the balls, squeeze his windpipe, try and gouge out his eyes.

I sometimes wonder why men don't try it on with me. Maybe I'm too ugly or too flat-chested (I think Sally has taken all the boob genes in our family). Pete says I don't need my self-defence lessons as I scare men off naturally. Maybe if I wait long enough, someone will come along who will love me for my mind.

14th June
Revision programme has gone to pieces. Fed up with taking

exams. Wish they were all over. Thank goodness my hayfever hasn't been so bad this year. Maybe the sprays have helped, or maybe there's been no pollen.

19th June

The big day! THEY'RE OVER and there's a party at Mark's house. Mary came round to get ready at 3 p.m. The party wasn't due to start till 8. She looked brill in her outfit. I was really jealous and had serious doubts about my new skirt, but Mary said it looked great. She's a good friend to have sometimes.

I tried some new lipstick—sort of dark rose colour—but it was too dark. I mixed it with some of the usual stuff and my lips ended up looking like a chocolate-covered raspberry. Talking about chocolate—I'm going on a 'no chocy' diet. I still weigh 56 kilos!

We got to Mark's just before 8.30. It was all Jungle and Hip Hop and I immediately wished I'd worn my 50Is. I felt a bit nervous as I couldn't see many of my mates, though some of Pete's were there, including Sam, so Mary and I went over.

Mary was all over Sam like a bitch on heat and I felt insanely jealous. I stormed off to get myself a drink—hotly followed by Sam, who gave me the 'What's up with you?' line. How could I possibly explain?

I picked up my drink and rushed off to the loo. When I came out, I came across Randy Jo and big-breasted Brenda heavily into business behind the settee. Not surprised Pete now thinks she's a slag. It's amazing she's not up the duff yet, the way she goes at it.

I sat under the stairs for half an hour drowning my sorrows in drink. Don't know why I drink—it's more a depressant than a stimulant, and what's more I feel rotten next day. While I was sitting there, someone I didn't know tried offering me an 'E'. No way was I going to try it. I think it's mental to use drugs like cocaine, heroin, and amphetamines. They should stay illegal to put people off using them. Though cigarettes and alcohol are drugs too—and I do use them. I think it is utterly wrong for people to make so much money from trades that are killing people and destroying so many lives.

Boys are full of such shit with their corny 'chat up' lines. This guy continued, 'Here's ten pence—go ring your mother and tell her you're not coming home tonight,' and 'Nice dress, think it would look good on my bedside table.' Told him to go get a life and that I wasn't hot for boys with bum fluff on their faces.

Then John came over to see if I was OK, and for some unknown reason (maybe the drink) I told him all about Sam. John decided I needed cheering up so he took me to meet a mate of his—Charlie—after I had checked the state of my mascara in the bog.

Charlie seemed a nice enough bloke, witty and not bad looking—the sort of dark-haired, blue-eyed bloke you'd give your last Rollo to. We talked about music, school (he's leaving this term), and how boring the town is getting. We actually had a lot in common (Stone Roses and Oasis) and I felt really relaxed talking to him. He didn't put on a macho-bastard image when his friends came up, which was a change.

A bit later he asked me if I would like to take a walk outside, which made me a bit nervous. Some boys seem to see this as an opportunity to stick their tongues half-way down your throat which can put a damper on the situation. I didn't want it to start getting heavy. But I felt no pressure from Charlie and he didn't even fumble my bra. He wrote down his telephone number and I gave him mine, but it will probably be a one-night stand—the kind of stuff dreams are made of. If he doesn't phone it was nice while it lasted, if he does I'll be over the moon.

21st June

He hasn't rung. Stupid of me to think he would. Wonder if I should give him a ring to see if he's lost my number? I'd look a right fool if he hadn't and doesn't want to see me again. Why am I so sad?

Actually, I'm not sure that I do want to see him again. From something Pete said yesterday, I think he may be into the drug scene, and anyhow he's got druff.

22nd June

Pact at school between Emma, Kate and me not to eat food that's bad for us. We're feeling lumpy after all that nervous eating over the exams.

Don't know what's got into Emma. She's stressed out at the moment.

26th June

It's all a bit dodgy with Emma. We knew something was wrong but not how rough things are. She did it with Mark at the party—went the whole way, the lot. What a way to lose it— under the influence at two in the morning when she couldn't get a lift home. And with that spinner Mark. She didn't let on till today, and now she's worried she's pregnant as she's a day late.

The whole thing was really mucky. Can't understand it—no condom—just spur of the moment stuff. Where's Emma been, for God's sake? She needs to grow up—but me saying all this is not going to help her now.

She knew a bit about emergency contraception but was too embarrassed to go to her doctor because it's the same one as her parents'. By the time she was really frightened, it was after the deadline. Now she's even talking 'abortion'.

27th June
So far, I've managed not to eat:

chocolate for two days

cake for four days

sugar for five days

cream for a week

I did feel like a whale, but I'm certainly not a minnow yet. Kate's lost 2 kilos—and she was only 45 kilos to start with. She says she wants to become a ballet dancer. If she's not careful, she'll become anorexic.

30th June
Emma's still not come on. She borrowed a fiver off me yesterday to buy a 'pee' pregnancy test. Took the bus into town so as not to be seen in the local chemist. She hasn't rung me yet. She should know by now as they give instant results virtually immediately after a missed period.

Emma rang—so far so good, it was negative. Kate's persuaded her to go to the family planning clinic to have it double checked.

Flab is in the Eye of the Beholder

2nd July

Emma's retest was negative! She's been given a load of condoms 'just in case'.

Dieting didn't last long. We've all stopped except Kate. We decided it was stupid, but she's become obsessed. She wouldn't come to Coles for a celebratory 'end of dieting' tea. She made a feeble excuse about meeting her mother, but I'm sure it's her not wanting to eat. According to Mum, Sal went through a not-eating stage for months, when she was doing her GCSEs, but it never got very bad. Mum dug out a booklet she'd got for Sally at the time.

Anorexia

Jenny's Story

I'm not sure how my anorexia started. All I do remember is wanting to be as thin as a friend of mine. I wasn't fat or anything. Just average size. But for some reason, I desperately wanted to be thinner, like my friend.

At this particular time—I must have been about 12—I became aware that my brother was thinner than me, though I didn't really start dieting properly then. My mother had always been fussy about what my brother and I ate—mainly because of our teeth. We'd never been allowed biscuits or cakes, just the occasional sweet. You see my father was a big fat man, and my mother thought that there was nothing worse than having fat children as well.

It was in my second year at senior school that I decided it was about time I was the same size as my friend. I can't actually ever remember waking up wanting to diet. It was just a very gradual process.

A year later I was seriously underweight and was diagnosed as anorexic. I was given a week to live if I didn't start eating. I had gone through several changes in my eating habits during that year.

I started off having fruit for breakfast, pork pie for lunch, and a small dinner. I took ages to eat each item as I deliberately cut it into tiny pieces, the same way each day. My meals had to be at rigid times, and any later or earlier would be terrible. I can remember distinctly cutting up my pork pie into very small pieces and sucking each tiny particle of meat. Then my breakfast changed to a small piece of melon, and lunch to a scotch egg. (It had to be a very special one, and if I couldn't get it there was trouble.) I started doing lots of exercises too.

Life was hell for everyone and I cramped the whole family's style. Going out for a meal was a waste of time and money, and not just me but *no one* enjoyed it. Then things got even worse, with no breakfast, a tiny salad with no chicken for lunch (my parents didn't know), and small pieces of cut-up vegetables for dinner.

The season changed and I remember getting really cold now that it was autumn. My parents became very worried. It was now obvious that something was definitely wrong. (I suppose they had realized that for a long time but hadn't wanted to accept the situation.) My mother feared that I might have anorexia, and said that if I wasn't careful I'd have to be fed by a drip into one of my veins. I got angry with her and told her not to be stupid. How could a person as fat as me be told to eat and put on weight? The fact that I was many kilos less than all my friends never made it click that perhaps I was actually very thin. I continued my regular exercises and went on refusing to eat. I suppose you could say I'd become trapped in a vicious circle and my anorexia had completely taken me over.

However, on 12th November I had to go into hospital. (I was 14 at the time and 163 cms. tall.) I weighed only 34 kilos, but I didn't want to go there at all. I didn't want any kind of help, though I do remember being made to have a small beefburger at McDonalds a few days before and thoroughly enjoying it. I hadn't had one for ages, and had forgotten how nice they tasted. However, there was no way that I was going to admit to liking it. My parents would have given me one more often and eating would have made me feel guilty.

When I arrived at hospital I was told that if I didn't put on 9 kilos by Christmas then I couldn't go home to spend Christmas with my family. Christmas meant a lot to me, and always had done, but my anorexia was so strong I didn't care whether I went home for Christmas or not. I just didn't want to put on weight. In the end I did go home—for Christmas Day only—as I had been successfully forced to eat.

In hospital I had to eat three big meals a day and three snacks with milky drinks containing a high-calorie powder. Eventually I reached my target weight and on 1st February was allowed home. I was relieved to be home again but my treatment continued, and I had regular family therapy meetings at the hospital as an outpatient, either with my family or on my own.

When I was diagnosed as having anorexia there were lots of different reactions from everyone. My family were shocked and upset. It was difficult for them to understand my eating problems, especially my brother who loves his food. What a lot of people find difficult to understand is that anorexics absolutely love food. They love it so much that they're scared that if they start to eat they won't be able to stop. But their anorexics' powers are so strong that they won't let themselves eat and enjoy food.

My grandparents found it tormenting too. They had never heard of the illness. They said it had not existed in their day. They found it so weird that I should want not to eat all the time. Even now I don't think they fully understand.

The only person in my family who is anywhere near understanding is my mother. She has had a mild obsession with food so it is easier for her to help me than most other people.

WHAT'S ANOREXIA ALL ABOUT?

Anorexia nervosa is a condition that occurs more commonly than you might think. It's not only girls who have the problem, but it is much more common in girls than boys. At least one in 100 teenage girls suffers from anorexia but only one in 2,000 boys. It usually starts in your mid-teens (it is much less common before the age of 13). Girls at boarding schools, fashion students, and ballet students are especially at risk.

There are lots of theories as to why it happens. For instance, it is an expression of depression, a response to stress, an attempt to run away from the conflicts of growing up; it's due to a feeling of being totally hopeless at everything; it's a fear of losing control over eating and becoming fat.

One common thread that runs through all these explanations is the stresses and strains being faced at this age by both sexes. The typical woman, for instance, is expected to be slim, beautiful, brainy, warm, loving, capable, kind, tough, business-like, etc.— ideals that a girl in her early teens may find rather frightening to live up to! To maintain control over at least one thing in her life— her weight—may therefore become an understandable obsession.

   One thing all anorexics have in common is that they all over-estimate in their minds how fat they are. Even though they may be thin and underweight, they *think* of themselves as fat.

WHAT ARE THE FIRST THINGS THAT HAPPEN?
* you lose a lot of weight by deliberately not eating and/or exercising a great deal
* you get obsessed with the idea that you are fat and it's a dreadful thing to be
* if you are a girl, you stop getting your periods.

WHAT OTHER THINGS CAN HAPPEN?
* your arms and legs become as thin as sticks
* your hands and feet become blue and very liable to chilblains
* you may not be able to sleep
* you may not be able to concentrate, though you may think you are being very clever
* you get very sensitive to cold
* your skin becomes dry and hairy over your neck, arms and legs
* your heartbeat rate slows down and down
* you may become increasingly sad and depressed
* you may become a compulsive user of laxatives (tablets which make you shit a lot and stop your food being absorbed, but which can also make you very ill).

YOU SHOULD WORRY THAT SOMEONE IS BECOMING ANOREXIC IF THEY:
* become obsessed with food and cooking for others, but don't eat themselves
* get very thin
* seem restless when meals are being served, won't sit down to eat with other people, and mess about with their food instead of eating it
* leave the table before meals are ended (often to spit the food out somewhere or make themselves sick in the toilet)
* spend all their time weighing themselves and recording all the details
* do very devious things and behave very secretively

* ✱ tell everybody that they don't have any problems, especially with their weight
* ✱ take huge amounts of exercise, often overdoing things
* ✱ wear clothes which conceal that they are in fact very thin.

IS THERE ANY TREATMENT?

At the moment we can't stop people from getting anorexia and there is a lot of argument over the best ways of treating it. However, most anorexics do get better, with only about one in three going back to having a problem, usually when they are under stress.

First though, someone has to recognize that there *is* a problem, and this is usually not the person who has got it. Secondly, the person who has got it has to be persuaded that he or she does need help. It doesn't really matter who gives the help to begin with—parent, teacher, friend. After that, the family doctor is the best person to go to, who may then ask a specialist at the hospital for more help. Usually this can be given by regular visits to hospital, but if the anorexic is very, very thin, he or she might have to stay in hospital for several weeks. This is because anorexia can be VERY dangerous. Some people die from the effects of starvation.

BULIMIA

Bulimia is another eating disorder like anorexia, and is sometimes part of it. At least two in every 100 girls have severe bulimia, and it most commonly starts around the age of 16. Although lots of people go through periods of chaotic eating, especially when they get stressed, bulimia is worse than that. It often starts with someone going on a strict diet, which is so restrictive that they can't keep it up. They then have an enormous binge—up to thirty times what they normally eat—and then make themselves sick, because they are guilty and frightened about getting fat.

Often these binges are again followed by going on a very strict diet. Sufferers yoyo backwards and forwards between dieting and eating masses. The best way of breaking into this cycle is to stop intense dieting and to eat small regular meals.

Mum says she read somewhere that if you put food on a very big plate it makes the anorexic think that they are eating a smaller portion than they actually are. Myself, I can't understand how people can starve themselves.

Ate three jam tarts with cream and a whole Yorkie after reading all this.

5th July

At last Pete seems to have found a proper girlfriend. It's Sandy (who used to go out with Randy Jo and is in the lower sixth). Kate says that her mum says that Sandy's dad is in hospital. I'm really pleased for Pete that he's found someone who likes him at last!

Whose *Job* is it Anyway? 10

6th July

It's strange not having to revise every day. Don't know what to do with myself. Dad says that Pete and I should now be doing ALL the washing-up and housework. Mum let us off during the exams. Parents shouldn't have children in the first place if they can't cope with it all.

I'm a bit scared of work experience next week. Sam's got a job with Pete unloading lorries at M & S. Wish I could work with him. That was my first choice. Second choice was trailing round with a barrister. Would have really liked to do this too— fancied the murder, sex and violence. John got it instead. Maybe he'll tell me all the juicy details.

Actually I'm pretty angry. What have I ended up doing? Working as an assistant in a primary school, where nearly all the teachers are women. It's blatant sexism, though Mr Rogers said it was nothing to do with sex but just happened to work out that way. Laughable hypocrisy again. At least Emma's doing it too.

7th July

Raining, nothing to do, fed up, miserable, hopeless. Reminds me of what I went through when I was 13. At that age I used to think I was the only one with the miseries, but then I found out that a lot of others had them too. Sometimes I would come home from school, go up to my room, and cry. I thought everyone and everything was against me, and I would have no social life or friends ever. I thought my parents didn't care, that no one cared. I would talk to my teddy or Bov, as they couldn't answer back like Pete always does.

I remember Mum saying, 'It's just your age.' If only I had known how right she was. I thought I was the only person in the universe who felt like that. Everybody else was blissfully happy, could do their schoolwork, and had friends they could talk to. At school we joke about it now and compare what we all went through—but I don't feel much like laughing and joking today. I tried watching *Dirty Dancing*, but even that didn't work.

8th July

Awful day. Mum said I couldn't go out unless I cleared up my room. I'm 16 and she treats me like a child.

9th July

Better—first day at work experience. The children are really sweet but a bit much. Me and Emma couldn't step out into the playground for fear of being mobbed on all sides by a thousand 5-year-olds. One little girl jumped on me from behind. She landed flat on her face on a step and cut her lip. I didn't know what to do. There was blood everywhere. Then the lady on duty turned up and took her off to the secretary's office.

It's a real ego-booster to have thirty children looking up to you. Also, it makes me feel good knowing I can teach them something. (So different from the constant put-down from my friends.)

10th July
Problems with the teacher I'm working for today. She started off giving me one specific thing to do. Then when she saw how much I was enjoying piddling around helping in the drawing corner, she lumbered me with a great box of pencils to sharpen. Emma's having the same problems. We both had blisters to compare at the end of the day. Also, the teacher gets angry if I get too friendly with the kids.

Mind you, from the way some of them look I'm not sure I wouldn't catch something from them. Classrooms are a prime breeding spot for nits, with the children working head to head and walking around with their hair touching. You can almost see the lice crawling across. Being infested once this year is enough for me, thanks.

11th July

Sent off by Mrs Joels to buy some labels for a project. The way some shopkeepers look at people my age is insulting. This one's eyes followed me everywhere. They think we're all shoplifting vandals. Wrinklies nick things too. Since when has being young meant you're a thief, a vandal or generally something less intelligent than a piece of pasta? They're also always on about how we use bad language and are 'damn cheeky—not like in our day'.

Mum's getting on my nerves more and more too. I'll ask her a simple question needing a simple answer and she'll give me a long lecture, which really gets me.

13th July

Glad to be out of the clutches of those pestering hands. Yesterday I just sat thinking 'don't touch me', but today I had to smile pleasantly while all my class kissed me goodbye and gave me cards. I enjoyed the variety of the work but I think next time I'll make it clear from the start that no children will be allowed to hold on to me. At first I was so keen to fit in I didn't realize the consequences of letting one of them sit on my knee. Now I'm just relieved to be rid of the demanding little voices and the stupid teacher, who didn't even say goodbye.

Pete's perverse. Doesn't want me to go to parties which he's going to, even if I'm invited. Think Mum must have said something about Brenda. I told Pete it was paranoia on his part. He hates it when I use long words. He bet me I didn't know what it meant, but I told him, 'It's thinking people are getting at you when they're not.' I am a Health Freak too! He thinks he's the only know all around, and says boys have bigger brains than girls. Told him yet again it's quality that counts.

Some people are leaving school this term—for jobs, training and unemployment. I'm furious because Sheila's dad won't let her stay on to do her 'A's. He said that girls don't need to get an education as they are just going to raise a family. Neo-Victorian Fascist.

16th July
Lovely letter from Charlotte who's still having a good time in Birmingham. I miss her a lot.

Dearest Honeybunch
Hope this gets to you before you go away. If it doesn't—bloody postman's on strike. Well, how did it go? What? Ha ha your intellectual ha ha work experience ha ha again. God, I am in a mature mood tonight. It's because it's the eve of my birthday, I guess—did you? I can see you shaking your head. I am not usually like this, am I???

Well, school has finished which is a relief. Then again, I've so much work to do—two art projects and a couple of lovely essays. But I wanted to get a job—a job at the local pub (yes—even though I am under age)—not the one down the road, but a bike ride away. I have seen some hunky blokes serving behind the bar there—know what I mean?

It was great talking to you on the phone the other day. I could hardly understand what you were saying though. So if I said the wrong reply to anything it was because I couldn't hear properly and was just saying 'yes', 'no', 'it's all right for some', which I usually say to my mum and dad when I'm not listening. Hope you have a great time on holiday. I'm going away in a couple of weeks which should be fun.

How is your non-eating sweets, cakes and crisps going? Given up have you? I can't get through a day without at least one piece of chocolate. I'm sure it's addictive. I'm going swimming every morning to get me and my body fit. Yes—even on the morning of my birthday. Wow Char, you're a star—how doja do it?

My brother's become a real pain—constantly being silly, saying wonderful things like, 'Char you've got hairs growing out of your chin, just like mummy.' Charming boy—I hate 6-year-olds. (So do I after last week's work experience.)

Well honey, I had better send this off—your bestest mate ever
Charlotte xxx

19th July

Brenda's passed her driving test. Pete thinks it's her tits that got her through. I hate the way boys talk about girls' breasts behind their backs.

Had a jab at school today against tetanus. Don't know why they couldn't have done it with the measles and rubella jab. I won't need another, and no lock jaw if I cut myself. Should have had it last year, but forgot to give Mum the form to sign (scared of the needle).

Had to line up with all the giggling Year 9s. 'Bet it hurts', 'Suppose I faint?', 'I feel funny already', 'Please miss can I have

it another time?', 'Cor, look at the size of the needle'. Don't know what the fuss was about. It only hurt if you knocked it a bit afterwards. Had a drop of polio stuff at the same time.

We've got to make our 'A' level choices tomorrow, when our sixth-form induction course ends. I haven't the faintest idea. Can't really decide till I know my exam results, can I? Pete suggested knitting, PE and French—I hope he's failed all his. Mum suggested biology, history and English and Dad suggested maths, physics and biology.

My physics teacher, Miss Boil, was helpful for once. She asked me what I thought I wanted to do as a job in the future. I haven't really thought. I used to want to be a vet during my 'furry animal' stage. During the last ten years I've wanted to be a racing-car driver, lawyer, woman priest, accountant, computer engineer, business woman, balloonist, explorer, jet pilot, actress, poet, novelist. Now I actually have to make some kind of decision, I can't.

I put myself down for physics, maths and English, but can change it later if I want to.

20th July

School ends today. Pete, Sam and two friends are driving up to Scotland in Sam's dad's second car. Some of us hardly even have a first one—Dad's has been on its last legs for five years. I'm desperate to go—would even put up with Pete. But no no no—no from Pete, no from Sam, no from Mum and Dad.

Hate Mum and Dad. I'm 16 now, and anyhow what do they think I'd get up to? Why don't they trust me? I would just have a great time—that's all. And it would be better than going to Wales with Mum, Dad and Gran.

Anyway, I couldn't really go as Marie is going to arrive from France next week. Hope we have more to say to each other than we did when I was there.

29th July

Marie's arrived par le Tunnel, et elle says le train was très quick in France and très slow in England.

It's not going to be easy. Pete's gone off to Scotland— sharing the driving with Sam, as he's just got his test. They set off down the road at 50 m.p.h., and screamed round the corner. Dad wondered whether he should have taken out a life insurance on Pete. Mum called him 'heartless' and burst into tears.

Summer **Love?**

1st August

Great summer holiday this:

Scribbling in the back of the car crammed between Gran and Marie and on the way to God knows where.

Gran's spare teeth in a plastic box nipping my neck.

Car's broken down twice already.

It's pouring with rain.

NOW stuck in a five-mile traffic jam on the motorway.

Bovril's been sick and stinks.

Marie's sulking because Pete's not coming.

I'm sulking because Marie's coming and Sam's gone with Pete.

Dad's sulking because Gran's coming.

Mum's sulking because Dad's sulking.

Gran never stops talking.

And all this for what?—two weeks in a caravan in wet and windy Wales.

Five hours later—and still not there. In fact we're not anywhere as we're lost. Mum insisted on a bit of 'culture'—a visit to Ironbridge, full of things that happened in the Industrial Revolution. Luckily I'd done a bit about it at school. Marie was bored stiff and spent her time in the coffee bar with 'a headache'. Found her chatting up some French-speaking hunk. First words she'd said since we set out.

Dad's in a bate. Usual complaint about women lacking the 'map-reading gene'. Sexist. I'm much better than Pete at finding my way around.

2nd August

Woke snuggled cosily against the ceiling. Bright sun beaming through a chink. Bov sitting on my head by my left ear. Pee and flush of Dad in the bog. Lovely smell of Gran making tea—a steaming cup appeared at the edge of my bunk. Groan from Mum for us all to shut up please. Marie like a collapsed jellyfish in the bunk opposite.

Just one small problem—I'm on again. Wonder whether Mum and Marie (Gran must be past it?) will get it too—all of us living so close together. It's our pheromones again. They cause it—so I read—all of us starting our periods together.

Am lying in my bunk writing this and reading Jilly Cooper's latest sex fantasy that Mum disapproves of but will still read from cover to cover herself.

Great not having to get up. Not so great not even being able to fart without the world knowing about it in this small space. Doesn't stop Gran though. Suppose she's got not to mind seeing that she can't control it. Privilege of the old. I couldn't get away with it. Wish I had a gas mask at this very moment—if anyone lights a match the whole caravan will explode. Will be driven to get up to get away from the smell.

Last time I farted pompous Pete had to notice. 'I do detect

you're expelling flatus at the distal end of your digestive tract. Couldn't you have eructated instead?' As usual, he had to go on about how my fart was partly all the air I swallowed because I talked so much and partly made up of methane and hydrogen sulphide gas from the bugs in my gut working on the food I ate. All in front of Sam too. 'You're just one large walking fart, being a vegetarian and insisting on eating so many beans.' He's a real fart-arse himself—knowing all the answers to everything—but I miss him on this holiday.

3rd August

Sun, sun, sun. Marie's got all the gear—sun glasses, before-tanning creams, tanning creams of every number, after-tanning creams, beach towel—the lot. Her bikini is about as big as four mouse droppings. Mum's horrified. Keeps saying how it's cold and shouldn't Marie put a jumper on. My bikini looks like an overcoat compared with hers, and I've only got

Mum's smelly old hand towel and a bottle of last year's suntan lotion.

Spent morning lying on the beach. We started with just us, and gradually became surrounded by white spotty bodies, all eyeing Marie, making remarks, and laughing like nerds. Then Gran arrived with a deckchair, vast knickers and hair bulging out of a bathing cap. She plonked down next to Marie and seriously damaged her sexy image.

Old people are really embarrassing sometimes. Not that Gran notices. She completed the picture by starting her knitting. She keeps nodding off—fell asleep in her soup last night. Gran says she can't help it—the doc says it's called narcolepsy. I say it's old age and so does Dad. Mum and Dad spent the morning in the caravan. Wonder what they're up to?

Marie seems different from in France. Her mum is like a real madame and is very strict with Marie. Now Marie's here she wants a mass rave and the cinema or a disco every night. Hope I'm not going to have to put up with her wingeing and pitying herself all the time.

By evening I was knackered by the sun but still dead white. I'd borrowed Marie's number 15 sun cream. I'm scared of getting skin cancer especially now there's this ozone hole over the Arctic, but this white is ridiculous. Number 10 tomorrow. Then I looked at my back in the mirror! Great red streak where I hadn't reached properly with the stuff—could even see my finger marks! Just when I wanted to start having a beautiful bronze body.

It's hard work having someone you don't know very well and don't particularly like crammed into this space. Marie said she was off for a walk before supper. Some 'walk'! When I went to get milk from the camp shop, there she was being chatted up by the greasos who were camping on the beach.

It's not that I'm jealous, or even fancy them, but I would like some kind of 'holiday romance'. Something I can tell Kate and the others about when I get back. After all, a bit of excitement is what holidays are all about. Kate always gets off with some incredibly handsome 20-year-old Porsche driver—or so she says. She lies about her age and thinks you can break all the rules on holiday.

4th August
Sun. Juggling act with Marie's sun screens today. Number 12 on most of me and number 15 on the parts which the other

screens hadn't reached. Asked Marie to rub it on my back, but one of her poncy admirers flounced over, took the bottle from her and started rubbing it in. I could've sunk into the sand and disappeared with embarrassment, but it was nice at the same time.

His name's Lee. He thinks it's great I'm a vegetarian, as he's a Green. He works as a lab technician in some place near Newcastle. We chatted in the café while Marie disappeared in the direction of the greasos' tents.

5th August

Sun. Met Lee on the beach again. His work's to do with a project measuring the radiation reaching earth from the sun. He's into how the chlorine from chloro-fluorocarbons is damaging the layer of stuff around the earth in the upper atmosphere called 'the ozone layer'. Just one chlorine atom mucks up 10,000 ozone molecules. He seems to know everything about it, and says the ozone layer is important because it mops up ultraviolet light before it reaches the earth's surface. This ultraviolet-B light is what causes skin cancer and the more that gets through, the more skin cancer people who are out in the sun will get.

Lee said the other problem is that people are sunbathing more nowadays. Luckily all the new high factor sun screens (15 or higher) help cut out the ultraviolet-B light. Most people in hot countries have always known to avoid being out in the summer sun between 11 and 3 o'clock. This is when the sun is at its strongest and can do the most harm.

I was getting dead worried till Lee said skin cancer doesn't really happen until we're older. He said I should think about it now though, because if I got a bad sunburn or had too much sun it would damage my skin and increase my chances of getting skin cancer when I'm older.

Mum is going spare about Marie. She's off all the time with the boys from the tents and Mum doesn't know what to do.

Must be worse when you're having to look after someone else's 'treasure'—as Aunty Pam calls me. Dad was called in to be heavy. Mum took Gran and me off to the café. I swear I could hear Dad shouting even from there. Marie is red-eyed. All her beautiful make-up was smudged when we got back. Dad said there was no need for me to be smug and I'd better behave or I'd get the same treatment. Total gloom and doom in the caravan. So much for holidays. What am I going to do about seeing Lee?

6th August

Rain. Has Marie got problems. The latest is spiders. I don't like them, but Marie goes spare. Mum says it's a 'phobia' and wishes it was a 'boy phobia'. A caravan is certainly no place for a holiday if you don't like spiders.

We all sat round telling one another about things people hate. Dad had read that Queen Elizabeth I hated roses. Freud, the headshrink, hated travelling, and King Edward VII wouldn't let anyone mention the number '13'. Hans Christian Andersen was afraid of everything. He was so scared of fire that when he stayed in a hotel he used to sleep with a rope around him so that he could escape. He was terrified of dirt too and washed his hands 100 times a day.

Dad thinks it's all a bit silly. In his job he's always meeting people with phobias about mice, rats, wasps, fleas, lice, spiders, beetles—in fact all creepy crawlies. He's also seen people cured. What they do is first get them to look at photographs of what they hate—say, spiders. Once they can manage that, they get them to pick up a photo. Then they get them to look at the real thing, stroke it with a pencil, and then actually touch it. I wouldn't fancy going to bed with a tarantula!

Gran had a friend who she called 'agoraphobic' because she couldn't go out of her house. She got treated in the same way. They took her to the door and just showed her the outside first, then took her a short distance, and then a little bit more each time she went out.

For Marie, it's not just spiders, she also has a thing about flying. Can't even bear going to the airport, let alone getting on a plane. 'Ze only time I flewed—my 'art it went boom, boom, boom, I breezed very fast, my fingers zey teeengled, my knees zey went to the jelly, my skeen it was like a pooooool of water.'

Dad's got a phobia because there's 'a great pooooool of water' on his bed where the roof is leaking.

7th August

Rain, rain, rain. Marie and I wanted to spend the day in the café (I haven't seen Lee for two days). But we were dragged off by Mum and Dad for some 'fresh air'. Marie thinks that the 'maladie Anglaise' is having picnics on the beach in freezing cold rain. We spent the rest of the day playing cards.

Another Leeless day, but it might have been him whistling at 11.30. I'm trying not to worry about my exam results.

10th August

Sun—and I've managed to see Lee at last. I'd gone with Marie to buy some ozone-friendly insect repellant and he was in the shop. Marie was already making for the tents, so Lee asked if

I'd come for a walk on the beach. I thought—why not? Might never get the chance again. You only live once. At least here on holiday I can turn up the sexiness a bit. At home I'd just be called a slag. He may not be the handsomest guy in the world, but he's here, he seems to like me, and he makes me feel good.

We sat (well, a bit more horizontal than sitting) in a hole in the dunes, out of the wind, and told each other about our lives, though I lied about my age and tried to sound experienced. I began to wish I hadn't when things began to get a bit heavy. I wasn't sure just how far to go. I certainly didn't want to go too far. After a while, I began to feel as if it was getting out of control, and I wanted to stay in control, thank you very much. Suddenly, I noticed a distant figure. It was Dad, which brought things to a very sudden halt. Snogging hasn't spoilt my feelings for Lee—though I'm not sure what he thinks of me now.

Got back to find Gran on the steps of the caravan, shaking out sand from her bri-nylon knickers which were covered with skidmarks.

If the article I read in Sally's copy of More is right—that every kiss takes three minutes off your life—I reckon I must be nearly dead by now. Feel exhausted and can't write any more tonight.

Hope Mum and Dad don't notice Marie's love bites, or mine for that matter. We were desperately trying to cover them up with make-up.

11th August

Sun, but it might as well be raining because Lee's going today. I saw him in the café. He hadn't told me he was off. He still seems to like me, took my address and promised to write.

Boring day. Don't know what to do now Lee's gone. Sunbathing's really pointless. All you do is get brown and then cover it all up because it's too cold. Anyway, people who live in hot countries have really wrinkled skin. I don't want mine to look like Gran's when I'm Mum's age. Mum asked what the matter was. Why does she want me to be happy all the time? I can't be. She isn't.

14th August
Going home tomorrow. The last few days have really dragged, but Marie's going straight back to France so I've something to look forward to.

Romance and Results

12

15th August

Home to Pete. So pleased to see him, gave him a hug. He pushed me off and told me to stop being emotional, though he was obviously pleased to see me. Why do boys find it so difficult to show emotion? Hope he's more affectionate with Sandy when he sees her again. Bov's OK on emotion. She showed she was pleased to be home and slept on my bed last night.

Turns out the boys got stopped for speeding, and breathalysed. They'd managed all the speed cameras OK but got done by an unmarked cop car. Pete was driving but he never even takes one drink if he's going to drive—he's much too afraid of losing his new licence. But he was driving at 83 m.p.h., so he made me swear not to dob on him to Mum and Dad.

No letter from Lee—surprise, surprise—but maybe I'm expecting too much. Even if I never see him again, he's turned me on to the idea of being a lab technician and doing something useful in life.

Sal's just back from a cheap package holiday to Spain with her girlfriend. Sal's boyfriend couldn't go because he had to work. They won't tell me the details of what they got up to. Said I was too young to know about that sort of thing yet. Must've been good though—they seem hyped up about it. I told them about my 'romance' so they showed me their 'Holiday Romance Survival Kit' which they'd found in a mag on the plane. Sal said that although the books were right in saying one had to be responsible and considerate, sometimes she just wanted to have a good time. In some ways she felt that was OK, as long as she was careful. I revealed to Sal that I was the author of the 'You, Sex and Contraception' article in the school newspaper. Think she approved.

Holiday Romance Survival Kit

1 Never give away something you might want back, whether it's a gold charm left to you by your grandmother, or your virginity.

2 Beware of moonlight, soft guitar music, sweet words, and cheap red wine.

3 Don't take anything back with you that you don't want. Unwanted pregnancies and sexually transmitted diseases, especially AIDS, are not easy to get rid of.

4 If you might need them, and if you don't know the Italian, Greek, Spanish, Turkish, French or Swedish word for condoms, take them with you. If your memory is bad, you're careless, or just not good at languages— remember emergency contraception. This can be used up to seventy-two hours after making love, but doesn't protect you against diseases. It is available in most European countries.

5 Never go back to the same place and expect your hunk to fall into your arms—he's probably in somebody else's.

6 Don't expect your feelings, or his, to be the same when you get back home. Holiday romances are holiday romances. One of the definitions of romance is that it's a wild and wanton exaggeration, very remote from the experiences of everyday life.

16th August

Pete got his exam results today, and managed to live up to his reputation. Two 'A's and a 'C'. He said what really gave him the piss was the 'C', as he had worked his bollocks off in chemistry but blew the practical—literally, as he actually set his experiment on fire! He was especially annoyed because Randy Jo got the same, and appeared to have done no work. Randy thought 'looking as if you worked' had no street cred.

Radically cool Sam sent me a postcard! which arrived today

too. Goodbye Lee, welcome back Sam. Wonder how he did?

20th August

Sandy's back from her hols now. Never see Pete. Either he's on the job at M & S or he's on the job at Sandy's. Mum's getting really manky with him. When he's not working, he never helps around the house and gets out of bed in time to watch Neighbours.

22nd August

My exam results tomorrow. Mum said she'd drive me down to the school as I'd 'forgotten' to send a stamped and addressed envelope.

1 a.m.—can't sleep. Rotten having 'brainy' Pete as a brother. At least Sal understands. Sure everyone's done better than me. Anyhow, I don't really care how I've done. It's not as if me failing my exams is the end of the world. There's a lot else in life—tell me about it. Mum and Dad have been good about not applying pressure, but I still feel they'd like me to do well.

23rd August

Well, this is it. Crunch time in ten minutes—must get up. Pete 'greased' me with a 'Don't sweat it honey, have one of mine,' as I left.

Yippee! It was OK—very OK, for me anyhow. All the way there I insisted to Mum that I'd failed everything as a way of protecting myself. Couldn't face going in myself, so sent Mum instead. She came out looking furious, and I thought, 'Oh no— that's it.' Then Mum burst out laughing—3 'A*'s (for drama, maths and history), 2 'A's (for combined science), 2 'B's, and 1 'U' (for French). At least that wasn't a surprise, though Mum wanted to go for a re-mark. No way.

Kate rang and asked about my holiday. Neither of us could quite bring ourself to ask about the other's results, though I was desperate to know hers. Pete, of course, said that it was just freaky marking. Don't think he likes competition from his little sister.

Dad's really pleased. At least *he* doesn't think that 'good looks' is all that matters in girls, though boys seem to think different. He'd seen a survey showing that what boys most admired in girls were: (1) good looks (2) understanding (3) warmth (4) honesty (5) loyalty (6) tenderness and only (7) intelligence. Independence, forcefulness and ambition all came last. When it came to what girls admired in boys, it was still good looks at number 1. Then: (2) understanding (3) honesty (4) loyalty (5) warmth (6) intelligence. Ambition, forcefulness and independence again came low.

What was really weird was that the same survey showed that what teenagers really cared about most was: (1) cruelty to animals (that would be me two years ago, but now I worry more about pollution—thanks to Lee—who still hasn't written) (2) unemployment (3) education (4) famine (5) racial discrimination and (6) nuclear war.

28th August

A lot of my friends are still away and it's starting to get boring, though I don't want the holidays to end. Everyone is surprised that I did as well as I have. Even Mary rang up to congratulate me. Generous of her as she failed three of hers. It's horrible of me, but I feel glad she did badly—she deserved to. She spends all her time out with boys. I know it's awful of me, and I know I'll probably regret it, but it's just the way I feel right now.

31st August

Looking forward to seeing all my friends and having a good gossip. Pete's worried because Sandy's dad is back in hospital with some kind of heart problem. He didn't know the right words to say to comfort Sandy.

Falling to **Bits**

13

1st September

Still haven't fixed my 'A' level options. Totally confusing. Why now? I hate making decisions. Seems as if the whole of the rest of my life depends on this one.

Back to school in three days. Can't face it. When I get fed up like this it's usually because I'm tired or bored, or about to come on, which I am. I looked in the mirror this morning and thought, 'God, you look like a frog'. Then I thought how pretty everybody else is. When I'm in this mood I usually bite somebody's head off—Mum's—she makes me the maddest. She treats me as if I was a child, and makes comments and jokes that I'd make to a 3-year-old. In her eyes I'm still a little girl, but in mine I'm grown up. I feel like an adult, and I want to make my own decisions without consulting her first.

Trouble is that in her day you were the age you were and that's how you felt, but nowadays you have the mind of a 20-year-old in the body of a 16-year-old. Mum thinks she's preparing me for a big bad world, but I know as much as she does about life, and in some ways more.

I've decided to write out a list of dos and don'ts for when I'm a parent.

I will:

✓ allow my children to choose whether they do what I want them to do, or not

✓ remember what it was like being 16, and try to be more sensitive and understanding

✓ be more trusting

✓ give them more independence

✓ treat them as equals and treat their ideas with respect

✓ say sorry when I'm wrong.

I will not:

✗ act like a teenager

✗ be patronising

✗ say things like 'you always . . .', 'you never . . .', 'you don't know how lucky you are', 'it's just your age'

✗ talk about my children in front of their friends

✗ compare them with their friends (unfavourably).

2nd September
Just can't write. Totally hopeless.

4th September
Back to school today. Great to see my friends again.

5th September
Can't stand it—the house is hopping with fleas. *Pulex irritans*, Dad calls them. Twenty species attack man, and it takes one to three weeks for the eggs to hatch after being laid. At least in this country they don't carry plague, or any other nasties. I hate Bov. If only she wasn't so promiscuous. I think fleas should be counted as a sexually transmitted disease. It

certainly is with her. I'm bitten all the way from my ankles to my knees, and look a real sight. Mum, Dad and Pete are all scratching.

It's always worst when we get back from the summer holidays. Dad says it's because the eggs hatch out in the warm wet weather. Of course, the family with a pest control father is the last to get treated. He keeps promising to bring his spray stuff home, but it's always 'tomorrow, tomorrow'. Like my flute practice (which is why I decided to give it up).

If I could have one wish at the moment, I'd wish they'd improve the food at school. It doesn't matter how many times

us vegetarians complain, nothing is ever done. I've got the girls on the school council to organize a questionnaire on what everyone eats and what they would like to eat. I think now we're in the sixth form, we should have more responsibility.

6th September

Pete's still working at M & S and is loaded with dosh. He's beginning to worry about going to Nottingham. He's not so sure now he really wants to do medicine. He wishes he'd taken a year off.

I'm still faking it—trying to smile when I'm actually in a pit. Can't put the bad things out of my mind. Anyway, I've at last decided on my A levels. I'm going to do sciences—maths, biology and physics. I got As for those subjects (so much for what Miss Boil said on my report!). And I still quite like the idea of being a lab technician, in spite of Lee not writing.

7th September

Can't face another two years of school, with the same people and the same teachers. Why doesn't anything exciting ever happen in my life?

8th September

Went round to Emma's. Not there. Her mum says Emma, Kate, Sheila and Mary—MY mates (I thought) have gone off to town. Never thought to ask me, did they? Ganging up against me. Pete says now I'm being paranoid. Spent afternoon crying and talking to Bov. Got to talk to SOMEONE.

9th September

My mates came round! Turned out they were buying me an Oasis CD yesterday because they thought it would make me feel better. They knew I was having a real downer.

We're all going through it. Kate says she's fed up with her body. It's not that she thinks life would be any better if she was slim, but her head would be less screwed up. If she diets, she just puts it back on again when she stops. She can cope with not eating till she gets her period, but after that she gets mad cravings. She can be very strict about her eating for a day or so and then something snaps and she stuffs her face with chocolate, chips, sweets, anything fattening. This makes her feel guilty and worthless, and she gets spots and headaches. She wishes she could develop anorexia nervosa, even though she knows it can be a deadly disease. What a stupid thing to wish for. From what I read in that leaflet, it sounds as if she's getting bulimic.

Thank goodness I'm happy with myself today and I'm not gross. If others aren't happy, that's their loss. Funny how moods come and go. When Emma felt she couldn't do the work they set her at school last term, she wanted to pack the whole lot in, and leave without taking the exams. Sheila's had it crucially bad. She will have to resit some of her GCSEs at evening class, and now she's worried she won't be able to get a job. She nearly got raped and didn't get much support from her parents, and now she feels she can't talk to them about anything.

During the summer, when she'd had a few drinks, Sheila nearly decided to kill herself, like Roger Simpson at St. Joseph's School last year. Nobody had realized he was depressed. He seemed to have everything going for him. He sat in his dad's car in the garage with the engine on. Really sad. Everybody felt guilty because they could've done something if only they'd known. After all, depression can be treated, just like any other illness.

Sheila rang the Samaritans. She got their number from the local phone book. She gave it to us—said, 'You never know.' They'd helped her a lot. They'd listened to all her troubles which made her feel better. They said they got 50,000 calls a year from teenagers, so she certainly wasn't alone. They'd suggested that if she couldn't talk to her parents, she should come and see them. They're open from 8 in the morning till 10 at night, and someone is around all night to take calls. Or she could go and see her family doctor.

I think I might choose to go and see my doctor, especially as they've just sent me a leaflet all about 'confidentiality'. It says that I can trust my doctor to keep totally private anything I tell her—even if I am under 16. I don't need my parents' permission to see her, and it even went on to say that they wouldn't tell my parents if I was having sex (I should be so lucky—Lee where are you?) or was on the pill—unless I wanted them to know.

Sal came in to see me this evening. She's very changeable. When she's got nothing better to do, she comes into my room and expects me to amuse her. She'll be nice to me and I'll tell her some of my problems, or talk to her about some boy or other that I fancy. But when she and her boyfriend come round, and I come down to watch telly or something, she tells me to push off. I've got just as much right to be there as her. More, as I live here. If I say that she starts getting nasty—telling her boyfriend everything I've told her confidentially. Then suddenly, like this evening, she expects me to be nice to her again.

Sal's boyfriend's mum works for the Samaritans. It could even have been her on the phone to Sheila. I told Sal about us all being down—Sal's been the same in her time. She'd got some gruesome facts from her boyfriend's mum.

- suicidal thoughts are much more common than threats or actual attempts, and about 1 in 20 boys and about 1 in 10 girls have suicidal thoughts at one time or another.

- actual suicide is rare before the age of 14. After that age about 5,000 teenagers per year attempt suicide, but most of them don't actually want to kill themselves. There are about 130 deaths among males aged 15 to 19, and 40 deaths among females aged 15 to 19 in England each year but many of these teenagers don't mean to kill themselves either.

- among all the attempted and actual suicides, there is a definite reason in 2 out of 3 cases, and no clear reason for the others.

- the main reasons for suicidal thoughts and attempts are: trouble with parents, broken homes, school work, worries about exam failure, fear of unemployment, and relationship problems with a boyfriend or girlfriend. In some cases it is a way of getting away from intolerable stress, and letting other people know how unhappy they are.

- main feelings that occur before some of the attempts are: anger, feeling lonely or unwanted, worries about the future, and—if depressed as well—feelings of hopelessness.

Sal said that when her friend was very depressed a few years ago, she became stroppy, bad-tempered, quiet and withdrawn. She was always tired, kept bursting into tears, and didn't want to be with anyone. She saw her family doctor and used up all his supply of Kleenex. He didn't seem to mind—he had boxes of them everywhere. He arranged for her to see a sympathetic person called a counsellor, and said that if that didn't help she might need some tablets.

None of this sounded like me. When I get depressed I listen to my Oasis CDs—which Pete says drives HIM to murderous rather than suicidal thoughts. I also cope by ringing up a friend and having a long chat—that usually cheers me up, by going out with my mates, or by reading a book. If I can't do any of those, I sulk till someone notices. Then I have a good moan and that makes me feel better too.

I suppose feelings of sadness are just part of growing up. It's only if they go on for a long time—or get very bad—that one should worry. If mine got very bad, I'd realize I was ill and would go and get some help.

12th September

We're all into words. Why are words so important I wonder? Why do they change, like fashions?

Sixties

Groovy, fab, ciao, happening, pad, boutiques, far OUT, gear, too good, way out, weird.

Seventies

Hassle, no problem, take care, situation, laid back, zoned, smashed, over the top (OTT), male chauvinist pig (MCP), scene, relate, being INTO something, not my bag, check it out, guy, heavy, trendy, great.

Eighties

Ace, cool, lush, peed off, veg out, gang bang, twat, mellow, chillin, wow, pucker, naff, hip, hunky, horny, posse, dig, groovy, brill, dead cool, fresh, eggy, gross, twerp, bimbo, snog, excellent.

Eighties and nineties

Wicked, doody, easy, all right, fab, chill out, hot, on the pull, how's it goin?

The Diary of the Other Health Freak

Nineties
Decent, sound, sorted, safe, kinky, vibes, rude, out to lunch, nice, maca, rude boy, sad, get a life, fit, dodgy, chill, babe, you're a star, hard, threads, sweet, slacker, spinner, rough, rank, stress, mad, shagged out, sucks, weird, get real.

Smart cockney
Know what I mean, bleedin', bloke, dosh, OK mate, right, triffic, down the boozer, ta, dodgy, a right Brian.

Drug street slang, old and new
Crack, grass, high, trip, billy whizz, speed, blow, ganja, uppers, amphet, snow, coke, smack, henry, skag, gear, score, buzz, ecstasy.

For those into sex
Copulation, intercourse, fucking, shafting, shagging, bonking, making love, having it off, screwing, making it, doing it, squelching.

Yuppy talk
Designer, divine, bliss, anything in French, frock, darling, filofax, fab, too too, totally, the market, upmarket, downmarket.

Street cred
It sucks, dude, bad, wicked, yo, sweet, Babylon, def, casual, crucial, dick, ruination, mellow.

Media, media
Cool, classic, style, hip, key, modern, directional, holistic.

God, what do I have to be depressed about—it's ridiculous:
- I have lots of really nice friends
- I do look somewhat better than a dish-rag
- hardly anyone is REALLY happy at the moment—they just kind of make out they are
- Bov loves me
- my exam results weren't half bad

❀ my parents really do care about me, even if we do quarrel quite a bit
❀ I've got an ace brother
❀ I'm better shaped than a balloon
❀ Sam speaks to me occasionally
❀ what more could I want?

Even if I don't feel totally part of the 'in' crowd and absolutely 'with it'—it doesn't matter. Sal says nobody feels like this anyhow. I bet that the future is going to be absolutely wicked.

Getting it **Together**

16th September

Our first day at the Bodyshack keep fit club at the local pool.
The Samaritans put Sheila on to it. Never dared go on my own
but now we're all going. We did a fitness test before starting
and had to answer some questions:

1 Can you walk briskly up and down a flight of fifteen stairs three
   times, and then hold a normal conversation without being out
   of breath? *Yes/No*
2 Can you do hard running on the spot for three minutes without
   getting tired or short of breath? *Yes/No*
3 Can you quickly step on and off a chair for three minutes
   without getting short of breath? *Yes/No*

4 Can you put your hands flat on the ground with your knees straight? Yes/No

5 How many press-ups can you do?
   0–5 5–10 10–15 15–20

Then they tested us. They told me I was good on stamina and suppleness but awful on strength. I only managed three press-ups. Bit embarrassing as I had said on the questionnaire I could do 10–15. We were lectured by a Russian athlete-type woman who must have been taking male hormones on her cornflakes for the last ten years—she was all hairy and muscle-bound—on the golden rules of exercise:

1 Get moving—find more active ways of doing the things you usually do, like running upstairs instead of walking.

2 Get fit gradually—it takes time. Make yourself sweaty and out of breath but not uncomfortable.

3 Exercise regularly—get into a routine.

4 Keep it up—you can't 'store up' fitness.

5 Enjoy it—make sure the activities are ones you like and can do regularly.

We must have been a sight—sitting in the sauna after an hour on the machines. All sweat and flesh, except for Kate who still looks as if she's come from a Third World disaster area. I enjoyed it. It's very sociable and a real laugh—all of us looking so gross.

Kate was there trying to do away with the two kilos of what's left of her body. Sheila was there because of the Samaritans and because she's not happy with her job. She wishes she was still at school, and we wish we had her money. She thought that she would find all the jumping around and being womanhandled by Russian athletes even more depressing—but actually she's much better. Mary was there because she wants to keep her body supple and in shape for the boys, and Emma thinks that if she looks good she's nicer to people.

Nobody there liked us because they're all fat, flabby, and forty and think we're taking the piss out of them. I don't somehow think any of us will be competing in the next Olympics!

17th September
Hardly made it out of bed this morning. Don't know how I got to school today. I ache in places I didn't know existed let alone had muscles in. I'm not sure about this 'getting off your bum' stuff.

20th September
Am I perverse or perverted? I think I'm becoming a 'Fitness Freak'. I haven't really thought about sport since I twisted my ankle before the 400 metres (when I was 13). Now I'm in the lower sixth where my teachers tell me I don't *have* to do it—I *want* to. But I don't want to do weedy little girls' sports like rounders and netball—boring, tedious, and going on for only three seconds at a time because of too many rules. I want to do violent sports like rugby—rampaging round the field getting really dirty, smashing people into the ground, and swimming around in the mud. Then going off and getting pink and clean in a shower and feeling really good afterwards.

Where can girls play rugby, except at posh schools costing £10,000 a year? I wonder why blokes like team sports and seem more competitive than women? Must be something to do with their hormones or their upbringing. I like competing if I win—it used to be the only thing that made me run. Otherwise I found it dead boring.

Pete's a pain at the moment, letting everyone down. He thinks he's 'in love' with Sandy. I think he's being stupid. He promised to come with me and Kate to the late night cinema yesterday. Mum said we couldn't go otherwise, in case we got attacked. I sometimes think Mum is being overprotective. Just because I'm a girl she thinks I'm automatically going to get mugged or raped. Pete was allowed out at night at my age. Then Sandy rang and asked Pete to go to the pub, and he went.

He's not going to have any friends left when it finishes between him and Sandy. He keeps letting them down. Kate and I told him girls hate boys who are doormats. Pete's acting like a member of a religious cult. I don't think it's love—I think it's sex.

23rd September

A session on the torture rack again but I'm definitely getting fitter. We were lectured once more by the hairy-bottomed monster, this week on the exercise value of the different sports:

- **Walking**—great for stamina but not so good for suppleness and strength. For all-round fitness, you need another sport as well.
- **Swimming**—excellent for strength, suppleness and stamina, especially if you use various strokes.
- **Cycling**—great for stamina and leg strength, but not so hot on suppleness.
- **Jogging and running**—a fun, free and quick way to get fit. Good for stamina but not so good for suppleness.
- **Badminton**—fun even for beginners. Good for stamina, flexibility and strength.
- **Tennis**—fun and sociable, and good all-round exercise.
- **Squash**—very exercising, providing good all-round activity. Warm up before you start.
- **Team games**—great for stamina and strength, and pretty good for suppleness. You don't have to be good to play.
- **Weight training**—helps tone up your body and keep you slim and supple.
- ***Do at least twenty minutes exercise three times each week to make you sweat—any kind.***

It seems you have to do an awful lot of exercise to work off the calories you put on by just drinking one pint of full fat pasteurized milk. To do that, I would have to:

walk for 76 minutes
swim normally for 60 minutes
walk fast for 54 minutes
play badminton for 48 minutes
run slowly for 47 minutes
cycle for 46 minutes

play tennis or do aerobics for 42 minutes
run fast or swim fast for 32 minutes
play squash for 22 minutes.

Pete said that making love was the equivalent exercise of running a mile. He should know. Suppose it must depend on how you do it though.

We did weight-lifting this week. I think the weights I lifted weighed more than Kate. Kate herself looked like a bent beanpole holding up Big Ben. Sheila's flagging. She thinks horse riding is more her style. She likes the feeling of power, and being taller and looking down on people. She also loves the 'Jilly Cooper' romantic image, but knows the real thing's different—smelly and sweaty with a lot of what she refers to as 'mucking out'.

24th September

Beginning to get upset again about Lee not writing and Sam not taking any notice of me. Anyway, Sam's about to disappear from my life. He's off to work his way round the world. He certainly won't be interested in ME after adventures in hot countries filled with glamorous, sexy women. There's too much pressure nowadays over having a boyfriend. Everyone seems to expect you to and when you don't, you begin to wonder what's wrong.

I'm beginning to lose my confidence. It starts with one thing, like whether I've got any friends, and goes on to another—my looks, my clothes. Everything begins to crumble. I'm always comparing myself with my friends. Sometimes I want to break out and be original but I can't. How can I explain it? There are times when I would like to buy something that other people would call unfashionable but that I like. It's at times like this that I really appreciate Pete being around. He's like having an extra friend, and it gives me a good feeling of security.

25th September

Bicycling to school's more fun now I'm fitter. I beat speedy Winston up the hill today. The good thing about cycling is that if you're not feeling competitive you can go at your own speed, and see things you don't see otherwise. The bad thing is the danger I suppose. I'd wear a crash helmet if it didn't make me feel such a trog. I still think the only way they'll get people to wear them is by making it compulsory.

26th September

Pete's out with Sandy again. He's meant to be getting things ready for university but seems to have a one-track mind. A whole gang of them are going to another pop concert, as if Glastonbury wasn't enough. They had a long pep talk from Sam's dad about the dangers of drugs. He said the police and the pushers were sure to be out in force—and not to expect him to come and bail them out if they got into trouble. As usual—I'm not allowed to go.

Sam's dad gave us all photocopies of an article on drugs. Typical that I'm given the menu and not allowed to go to the feast. Anyhow, here it is:

Warning—drugs and being involved with the police can be harmful to your health
Remember—you don't have to join the drug scene to be part of the 'in' scene

Cannabis (weed, grass, ganja) Gets you up to five years for possession. Commonest illegal drug in the UK. Comes in different forms: as a resin which is smoked or cooked in food, or as a leaf which is smoked with tobacco. Effects include relaxation and making your senses (taste, hearing, sight) more acute. Doesn't cause a hangover and is not addictive. Does, however, reduce concentration, makes short-term memory worse, and very occasionally can cause acute confusion. People who smoke it all the time aren't called 'dope heads' for nothing. Other bad effects are that if you already have, or are susceptible to, mental problems it can make them worse; and smoking cannabis has many of the same long-term dangers as smoking tobacco.

Ecstasy (E, MDMA, ice, XTC, discobiscuits) Gets you up to seven years for possession. Known as the 'rave' drug and is being used by thousands and thousands of people. Peddled as a safe and OK drug —which it is NOT—and most of what is sold as ecstasy contains aspirin, dog worming pills, and a million other substances as well. The effects of genuine E (if anyone ever gets any!) are to make users friendly, energetic and generally delighted with their lot. Can also sometimes cause mild dizziness and nausea, and no one is certain yet about the long-term effects on your brain and liver. What's really problematic is the occasional death among people using E, which appears to be associated with the drug giving the impression that you can 'rave' for ever. This leads to exhaustion and dehydration due to sweating so much—and that can cause sudden death.

Amphetamines (speed, uppers, sulphate, wizz, billy) Up to five years for possession. Made artificially and like E is usually sold with a whole lot of other crap in it. Sniffed, swallowed, smoked or injected—but injection is very, very risky. Sniffing damages your nose, and rubbing it into your gums makes your teeth fall out. Makes you feel powerful, self-confident and energetic. In the long run, the effects of using the drug are tiredness, depression, and acute feelings that

people are getting at you—quite apart from the damage it does to your body.

LSD (acid) Up to seven years for possession. Trips can be wonderful or absolutely terrible, partly dependent on your mind state when you take it. Very occasionally people have jumped out of windows and done very foolish things while on it. Totally artificially made substance giving you an 'out of body' experience. Effects can take twenty-four hours or longer to wear off. Can cause acute anxiety.

Cocaine and Crack (coke, charlie, snow, freebase, rock, wash) Up to seven years for possession. Crack is a form of cocaine that is becoming popular. Both are bummers of drugs and exceedingly addictive. The effects (very fast and short with crack) make you feel really great. You need and want more and more to get that great feeling back. If you have to do drugs—DON'T do crack.

Heroin (skag, junk, smack, gear, brown) Up to seven years for possession. Comes from the poppy—but not the kind you get in England. Smoked, sniffed or injected. Often very impure. Makes you feel relaxed, happy and content. Highly addictive. You feel rotten when you can't get it and it's another one *NOT to do.*

Glue and gas sniffing Not at all a good scene, with two deaths a week in the UK and the threat of brain, liver and kidney damage. There are more than thirty substances around which give you an altered mind state through sniffing. One of the main dangers is doing something really stupid while under the effects.

Remember again:
—if you do experiment—know what it's all about
—at all costs stay away from injecting: the drugs are likely to be impure and you are highly at risk of getting AIDS

27th September

I've lost the key of my cycle lock, so I left my bike at school and walked.

The pop concert trip nearly ended in disaster with them all in jail. Turned out Sam's dad—after all his lectures, and unknown to them—had forgotten to take his medical bag, containing drugs like heroin and morphine, out of the boot of the car. He'd left his mobile phone behind too. The police had stopped them near the concert for a routine check. The sniffer dogs were just about to start in when a psychedelic van whizzed past and got stopped and searched instead. It wasn't till they got back that they realized what a near miss it had been!

Pete said that there were dealers sidling up all the time, trying to sell crack, cheap. He wanted to smash their faces in.

28th September

Still no bike, but I have the key. Found it this evening in Bov's basket. How did it get there?

29th September

Bike, key and lock all together at last. Collected bike from school in spite of the fact it's Saturday. Pete tore himself away from Sandy to drive me down in Dad's car.

All my pals are coming round this evening for a 'gathering'. (No, Mum—it's not a party.)

30th September

Was struggling out of bed after last night's home rave to go to the keep fit club—aerobics this week—when heard sudden scream of anger from Mum. She's cracked at last. Is this the end of the 'rave' age?

Why was the milk out of the fridge?
Why was there no bread left?
Why had all the lights been left on downstairs?
Why was the toilet blocked with paper?
Why was the kitchen floor covered with crisps?

Why had the apple pie that was for Sunday lunch been eaten?

Why did everyone use the ice-cubes and put the ice-cube tray back empty?

Why had three glasses been smashed?

Why did no one ever change the lav rolls?

Why did no one ever clean out Pinko's cage?

Why had no one fed the cat?

Why was the sink full of washing up?

Why did no one ever put their own dirty washing into the machine?

Why was the bottle of Jamieson's whisky all drunk?

Why was there a cigarette burn on the back seat of the car?

Why, if everyone must have take-aways, did they have to block the safety-belt slots with lettuce and tomato slices?

Why was the back door left unlocked?

Why were there three strange bicycles in the hall?

Why was this house such a pigsty?

Pete didn't seem to think there was a problem—which didn't help Mum's mood. Dad stayed out of the fray and in bed most of the day.

Never made it to aerobics, unless you count clearing up at home as aerobic exercise. Mum said I'm not missing anything as long as I take some exercise and today she'd rather it was at home—thank you very much.

15

Death, Dreads *and Drama*

1st October

Pete's in the dumps, getting at me in particular and the world in general. He referred to the human race as 'a foul genetic mistake'. Told me to 'grow up'. Informed me that I seemed to think that all there was to being mature was being aged 16, being able to make love legally and get married, making decisions about 'A' level choices, being able to have a conversation of more than three sentences, and now being allowed to stay out till midnight by Mum and Dad. He thinks that his extra two years' experience makes all the difference. He's so bloody patronizing—worse than the boys at school. Old 'know all' doesn't even know about women maturing earlier than men.

Anyhow, he and Sandy are pathetic—going around together like an old married couple. I suppose it's because he's about to go off to university.

2nd October

SANDY'S DAD HAS DIED. He had another really bad heart attack at work yesterday. He was rushed off to the hospital but was DEAD when he got there. Pete doesn't know what to do. Whether to ring up, whether to go to the hospital, whether to go and see Sandy at home, and what to say to her and her mum. Mum says he must go and see her. There's nothing worse than people avoiding you when disaster happens. That's what friends are for—to be there. She said it is bound to be difficult but emotions are something you have to face up to.

Pete came back later. He said Sandy had cried a lot but had been really pleased he'd come. Him just being there had helped her, even though it was a bit awkward at first. Sandy doesn't seem to be able to believe it's happened. She still expects her dad to walk in at any moment. Pete wants to talk about it. It feels so different from when Jason's dad died last year. Pete had found Jason in the pub the same evening, as though nothing had happened. Strange, the different reactions to death.

5th October

Hate the idea of Mum and Dad dying. It really frightens me. Don't think I slept all night, worrying.

Pete went to the funeral. He's convinced they are a good thing. Not that he'd enjoyed it, but he was able to say 'goodbye'. He thought that Mum had been wrong, not letting us go to Grandad's funeral for fear of upsetting us. Even Sandy's younger brother, aged 5, had been at the cremation. I think Pete's right because I still don't quite feel Grandad's gone. His was a heart attack too. I keep seeing people who look like him, and my heart sort of sinks each time.

In spite of all the sadness, Pete looked a real laugh going

off in Dad's dark suit, Sam's too-big black shoes, and awful Uncle Bob's black tie.

Pete's got himself a donor card. He doesn't want to be flattened by a passing car without being useful to the human race. There are hundreds of people waiting for kidney transplants, corneal transplants and heart transplants (and me for a brain transplant, he says). Once he's dead, he doesn't care what happens to his body. He gets angry with me when I say I don't want to have surgeons arranging for bits of me to be walking about inside other people when I die.

Couldn't sleep again. Came down at 2 a.m. to make Ovaltine, and found a convulsed Pete listening to the phone. He couldn't sleep either (he called it 'insomnia') and was trying all these numbers he'd found in a magazine. So far he'd phoned for information on:

> **What is an orgasm?**
> **Masturbation—the facts**
> **Is it wrong for me to dream about sex?**
> **Can love be just lust?**

The numbers had all been engaged. Now I know what insomniacs do at 2 a.m. All Pete could get through to was 'Girls' Bodies'. Couldn't think why he was laughing till I rang 'Boys' Bodies' and discovered. A disembodied voice told me of all the hidden treasures I could find inside boys' boxer shorts. What a load of toss. As for masturbation, from what I've heard, 90% of boys admit to doing it and the other 10% are liars.

I'm not sure what Dad will say when he sees his itemised telephone bill if I do this every night!

6th October

Exhausted. Pete insists that *he's* like Napoleon, Margaret Thatcher and Churchill, and can manage on four hours' sleep a night. Hadn't noticed this myself.

Pete had another go at Dad about smoking today. It worries him that Dad might get cancer or have a heart attack. At least he's not smoking as many as he used to.

I don't think I'll have any more arguments with my parents. What if they died suddenly and I was never able to make it up to them. I would feel that it had been my fault, and that God or whoever was punishing me and teaching me a lesson. Couldn't get to sleep for hours, for the third night running.

7th October

Held my older brother's hand when he went to Nottingham today! I knew he needed me as Sandy couldn't go, but he gave the impression of wanting to get rid of me and Mum as soon as we got there.

I want to go to university. There are condom machines in all the loos, so life there must be really fast. Think Dad tried to give Pete a packet before we left, as there was a sort of scuffle in the hall with Pete looking dead offended.

9th October

Sandy came round. I was terrified I might giggle out of

nervousness so I gave her a big hug. She burst into tears and I knew I was going to sob too. She's having to be strong, and try not to cry in front of her mum. Being the eldest, she feels she has to be responsible and support her. She said she keeps wondering what she's done wrong in life to deserve this. She goes over it again and again.

10th October

Got smashed by Emma at squash today, but it was a good game. Sandy's dad's death has made us all morbid. While banging around the squash court, Kate told me that she had had a sister who died when Kate was 5. She's never talked about it before, partly because her parents had been so stupid. They'd never explained to her what had happened, and now tried to pretend that her sister had never existed. She'd gone through sheer hell when it happened, and had felt totally and utterly depressed. No one could cheer her up, no one could understand what she was going through. Her parents had said, 'Time will heal.' Although that was true, it had been the last thing she had wanted to hear then. She remembered one day when one of her friends had tickled her to cheer her up. Instead of laughing, like she usually did, she had burst into tears, and everyone had felt embarrassed.

11th October

Sandy's back at school. We're trying to be really nice to her, and really considerate, but some people don't know how.

12th October

It's just like when I had my exams. I'm not sleeping a wink at night and I'm even missing Pete. Mum's sympathetic and says lots of things can cause it, like anxiety, stress, depression, overwork, or sadness at someone dying. Dad says that most people who think they haven't slept a wink have been found in experiments to actually go to sleep twenty minutes after going to bed, and then to sleep for a good six hours. Trouble is, that's not the way it feels to me. I lay awake *all* last night, worrying I was not going to get to sleep.

14th October

Still not sleeping properly. Mum said she'd find me something to read about insomnia, and that sleeping tablets were certainly NOT the answer as they are all addictive.

At least I've got Bov to keep me company, though Mum doesn't like her sleeping on my bed let alone in it. Bov knows it. If Mum comes in at night, she's under the bed in a flash. Bov and I really understand one another. She never answers me back, unlike some people in this house. She's been 'my' cat since Sal moved out. I sometimes wonder whether I'd mind her dying more than a human.

15th October

Terrible noises last night. Doesn't help my sleep problem, being scared to death. I decided it was Dad snoring, till I looked in the garden this morning. Bov's killed Pinko. I'm going to kill Bov next time I see her. Why can't cats be vegetarians?

Pinko went alongside the other eight graves—two hamsters, three rabbits, a mouse, a gerbil and Gran's budgie. I'll have to give up looking after animals. Care was needed with the grave digging as I wasn't sure what manky remains I might come across.

I hope cemeteries are more organized. Personally, I don't fancy being charcoal grilled and ending up as a little pile of grey ashes like Sandy's dad. I want to go into the ground whole—like Pinko. Dad disagrees and thinks that it is ridiculous using large parts of the countryside for burying the dead. He said it's much healthier and nicer to be cremated. Still, at least we have the choice!

16th October
At last Mum's got the stuff on how to sleep. It was in the Sunday paper. (Thought for the Day: 'Does everybody tear the cardboard roll of the toilet paper and use it when the paper has run out? If the answer is 'yes', then why don't they make it softer so it doesn't hurt one's bum so much?')

TIPS FOR NON-SLEEPERS

The bit of your body which most needs sleep is your brain. Everything from your neck down can do without it, provided it gets regular rest and food.

Even your brain, on average, only needs six hours' sleep a night, but this does vary from person to person. There appear to be two main kinds of 'sleep'—'vital' or 'deep' sleep and 'optional', 'light' or 'rapid eye movement' (because your eyes move rapidly backwards and forwards behind your closed eyelids) sleep. The second kind of sleep is when you dream, the first kind is the kind that revitalizes your brain. Short sleepers are able to miss out on 'optional' sleep but not on 'vital' sleep. Feelings of 'sleepiness' are what finally tell us whether we are getting enough sleep or not.

Some things to do:

1 Accept that *whatever* sleep you can get is going to be really enjoyable.

2 Try to go to bed at a regular time, and set an alarm so that you don't get anxious about waking up on time.

3 Don't indulge in weekend sleep binges.

4 Try relaxation exercises, or a brisk walk, in the hour or so before bed.

5 Don't indulge in heavy meals, Coca-Cola, alcohol, tea or coffee (unless decaffeinated) just before going to bed.

6 It's worth trying a glass of warm milk, hot chocolate or Horlicks.

7 Make sure your mattress and pillows are comfortable and the bedroom is not too hot or cold.

8 Pee before going to sleep.

9 If you can't get to sleep—don't toss and turn—get up and go and do something in another room. You don't want to associate your bedroom with sleeplessness.

10 Try relaxation tapes that are available in some shops.

Oh, well—can but try.

Food, Glorious **Food**

17th October

Something had changed when I woke up this morning. I'd slept! Waking was like swimming to the surface of a deep dark pool—up and up and up. Maybe it's because I think I just *might* have a boyfriend, at least I hope I have. I'll wait before I write his name down—it's such an embarrassing name and things might go wrong.

18th October

I'm fed up with being an only child so used £1 of my money to buy my own National Lottery ticket—it could be me and £12,000,000. IF I WIN I shall buy Sam's body for my own uses, Dad a Merc, Mum a trip to a health farm, and I'll give most of the rest to Oxfam and Save the Children. I'm not sure I'll buy Pete anything after his last effort at buying a ticket.

19th October

My wish about school food has come true, or maybe it's
POWER at last. Our 'questionnaire' has worked. The school's
into 'NEW-LOOK, HEALTHY EATING', with a typical, massive
'Let's all do this together' type programme. Gym, geography,
social studies, sports, a healthy eating 'word search' in the
school magazine—even the dinner ladies are involved. Anyhow,
they said they're fed up with making custard and jam pudding.

F	W	H	O	L	E	M	E	A	L	B	B	D	P
N	V	O	T	Z	N	P	E	A	S	A	R	O	C
U	L	E	N	T	I	L	S	F	A	N	O	U	E
N	K	T	G	O	T	F	A	P	P	T	W	G	L
S	C	P	C	E	U	F	I	S	H	A	N	N	E
A	H	U	E	Q	T	L	C	B	U	A	B	B	K
T	O	L	P	A	B	A	F	S	R	N	R	O	Y
U	N	L	E	W	R	N	B	O	I	E	E	T	C
R	L	E	Q	R	K	U	E	L	C	L	A	T	R
A	A	T	O	M	A	T	O	C	E	D	D	L	I
T	F	T	D	A	P	O	T	A	T	O	P	N	S
E	T	U	H	T	P	L	U	M	S	M	I	N	K
D	E	C	A	Z	L	C	C	E	R	E	A	L	U
A	K	E	L	P	E	K	I	L	S	E	U	M	T

The boys on the school council hate us. They've been to see
the head. They even arranged for the local chip van to visit at
12.30. Maybe it's because it sells fags—one at a time—as
well. Seems that smoking and unhealthy diets go together.

I'm really proud of our survey. We got the whole sixth form
to think out the questions, give out the questionnaire, and
analyse it on computer. Only blot on the landscape was the
one we gave to the staff. They won't let us analyse that—will
they?

Analysis of 'Healthy Eating' Questionnaire

Question 1
(a) Do you think the food provided by the school is healthy?
Yes—40% No—60%
(b) Do you consider the food you eat at home is healthy?
Yes—80% No—20%

Question 2
What are your favourite foods?

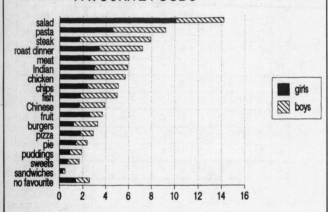

FAVOURITE FOODS

girls
boys

Question 3
Are your favourite foods available at school?
Yes—20% No—80%

Question 4

How often do you eat chips?

CHIP CONSUMPTION

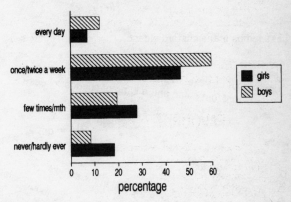

Question 5

What food do you eat in school?

FOOD IN SCHOOL

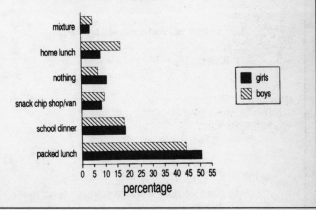

Other Comments You Have about Health and Food in School

Don't eat the food.

They shouldn't let local shops sell fags.

Less lumps in the custard please.

What about us vegetarians? Let's have more variety—instead of just salad and a lump of cheddar cheese.

Raise the age you can buy fags to 18.

Why only white rolls?

Why do all dinner ladies look like jam rolls?

Why was Doreen's toe-nail in my salad?

More choice please—what about Indian and Chinese foods?

Unbruised apples please.

Lots of fruit but no tarantulas please.

Can we have more chips please?

Get someone to turn the water into beer.

Cut out the grease!

Tidying the school up might help.

Why can't we have more West Indian food, man?

Glad it's worked. We now have baked potatoes, wholemeal rolls, vast salads of every variety, and nice fresh fruit. Not thinner dinner ladies though! They still look like jam rolls.

21st October

OK—his name is 'Willie'. He's 1.65 metres tall, blond haired, very attractive, in the upper sixth, wears really cool shirts, smells great and apparently is a good kisser and dancer, though Sandy says he's a bit of a stud.

Thank goodness Pete's away and doesn't know about him or the remarks would start. Willie has started coming to the Sports Centre on Sundays and we walk home together, but my friends are always with us. He says he'll help me baby-sit on Tuesday.

23rd October

'Thought for the Month'—I HATE MEN. They only think of one thing. I got Mum and Dad's permission for Willie to come and baby-sit with me at Mrs Smith's. Dad gave me a lecture on 'reputation' and stuff. Because I'm the youngest he can be very protective.

Anyway, Willie came round and after the children had gone to sleep we sat snogging for quite a long time. Then he pushed me on to the floor and asked me to have sex with him! I said 'NO'—though deep down I quite wanted to. I really fancied him, but I've only known him for two weeks. He kept on and on about it, but I still said 'NO'. He asked me, 'Why not?' I told him that it wasn't that I was scared, but that I'd never done it before, wasn't about to now, and at my age didn't relish the idea of getting pregnant. He gave me some bull about boys under the age of 18 not being able to get a girl pregnant—he must have thought I was really thick and piss easy. He also can't have read my ace article on sex and contraception in the school newspaper. He must know the facts—he's been to the same sex education classes at school as I have. Most boys have active sperms at 13. He went on to tell me he wouldn't pack

me in, and that he really loved me. Yeah, I thought, keep talking. But I wasn't going to give in, and in the end he left.

After he'd gone, I felt pretty cross. Being a virgin means something to me. I'm not just going to throw it away with ANYONE.

25th October

Yesterday Willie got his sister to phone and tell me that he didn't want to go out with me any more. I didn't feel upset. I kind of knew he'd do something like that. I was just really angry he hadn't had the guts to tell me to my face. At school now he's spreading rumours that I'm tight and can't kiss, and says he isn't going to bother with a frigid cock-teaser like me. Boys like that just aren't worth knowing.

There is a problem though. Sleep with a guy, you're a slag—don't sleep with him, you're frigid.

I told Mary a bit about it—though not the juicy details! My friends have nicknamed him 'Mini Willie'. They say he's probably got his big muscles—not because he ate the right foods and did the right exercises—but because he used anabolic steroids like they do in the Olympics, even though anabolic steroids give you 'deformed genitals'. Serves them right!

26th October

No lock, no bike now—just a key. Daren't tell Mum as I never got round to buying the combination lock. Just said I felt like a walk. 'It's good exercise, Mum.'

Geek at school, who's self-appointed leader of the 'chip and fag' gang, came up to me in the common room and said, 'I don't believe what you say about fatty foods giving you a heart attack when you're older. My grandad is 85 and has always eaten lots of greasy food, and smoked twenty fags a day.' I told him to clean out his ears. What I had said was not that fatty foods and smoking WILL give you a heart attack, but that eating fatty foods and smoking makes you much more likely to get a heart attack.

I thought Mum would have a heart attack when I got back and told her about the bike. But she already knew! How do they always know before you even tell them? Another thing that must come with 'maturity'.

17

An Aid to **AIDS**

2nd November
Relief. Half-term this week. It's given me time to recover. What is it about me and boys?

5th November
Nobody's having fireworks this year. Too many accidents last year, and anyway Dad says fireworks cost too much. I'm disappointed. Bet we'd have them if Pete was here. His accident a few years ago hasn't put him off what he calls 'being a pyromaniac'. Sounds a bit like being a hypochondriac.

We all went to the public fireworks in the park instead. Much better fireworks, but I hate the bangs, and I had mud up to my waist when I got home. There was jazz, and hot dogs—but also crying babies and smoke.

I spotted John, with Charlie—both lit up by one of the fireworks. I hadn't set eyes on Charlie for nearly five months! I nudged Kate—who dropped her toffee apple in the mud, and a dog licked it. I didn't think they'd seen us, then I heard John shouting my name. Charlie didn't seem to want to look at me and kept scuffing his shoes on the ground. He explained that he'd lost my phone number, and that HE was waiting for ME to phone HIM. He'd been too shy to ask John for it, in case I didn't want to see him again. I scrawled my number with Kate's eye-liner on the back of my new copy of Just Seventeen, and told him not to lose it this time.

6th November

The excitements of yesterday made me completely forget what was happening today. A trendy doctor at assembly gave the whole sixth form a questionnaire. She said she wanted to know what we knew and felt about AIDS. I thought it would be all about who I was going out with. Everybody else scribbled away, so I thought they must all be doing amazing things when I wasn't even going out with anyone—(yet?).

Sita Beegam's parents wouldn't let her fill it in. She's really nice, but she's not allowed to do anything with us. She isn't allowed out in the evenings at all, and her parents won't even allow her to attend PSE lessons, let alone the school Christmas party. Although Sita knows her parents are like that because they were brought up that way, and they think it is best for her too—she doesn't think they understand what it is like nowadays. How is she meant to learn about relationships and sex and stuff? Her parents say that they will arrange who she marries when she is old enough. At least they've allowed her to stay on and do her 'A' levels.

I'd run away if it was left to Mum and Dad to choose my husband. I hate to think what 'parent pleaser' they'd select.

What do you know about AIDS?

PLEASE FILL IN THIS QUESTIONNAIRE
The answers will be given to you later

How old are you? . . . .years. . . .months

Which sex are you? male female

1 **What does A. . . . . .I. . . . . .D. . . . . .S. . . . . .stand for?**

2 **What causes AIDS?**

3 **What does H. . . .I. . . .V. . . .stand for?**

4 **When was AIDS first discovered?**
1950–1960?
1960–1970?
1970–1980?
After 1980?

5 **How and where did it start?**

6 **Roughly how many people in the UK have the AIDS disease?**
1,000   5,000   10,000   100,000

7 **Roughly how many people in the UK have already died from AIDS?**
50   700   1,200   7,000   12,500

8 **If you get the AIDS virus, is there a test which can be done straight away that will show you whether you have got it?**
Yes/No/Don't Know

9 **If you get infected with the AIDS virus, does the infection last for the rest of your life?**
Yes/No/Don't Know

10   **If you get infected by the AIDS virus, do you get ill with it immediately?**
Yes/No/Don't Know

11   **Do all people infected by the AIDS virus die from it?**
Yes/No/Don't Know

12   **How do you know that you have got the AIDS disease?**

13   **Is there a cure for AIDS?**
Yes/No/Don't Know

14   **Can the AIDS virus be passed on even if you don't know you have it?**
Yes/No/Don't Know

15   **In a person who has been infected by the AIDS virus, where will the virus be?**

in their skin	Yes/No/Don't Know
in their faeces (shit)	Yes/No/Don't Know
in their saliva (spit)	Yes/No/Don't Know
in their semen (sperm)	Yes/No/Don't Know
in their tears	Yes/No/Don't Know
in their urine (pee)	Yes/No/Don't Know
in their blood	Yes/No/Don't Know
in their vagina	Yes/No/Don't Know

16   **How can a person catch the AIDS virus?**

by touching door knobs	Yes/No/Don't Know
by sharing dishes and glasses	Yes/No/Don't Know
by sharing toothbrushes	Yes/No/Don't Know
by sharing needles to inject drugs	Yes/No/Don't Know
by using lavatory seats	Yes/No/Don't Know
by giving the 'kiss of life'	Yes/No/Don't Know
by wet (french) kissing	Yes/No/Don't Know
by droplets of saliva	Yes/No/Don't Know
by anal intercourse	Yes/No/Don't Know
by holding hands	Yes/No/Don't Know
by touching an infected person's blood	Yes/No/Don't Know
by blood transfusion	Yes/No/Don't Know
by head lice	Yes/No/Don't Know

by mother to unborn baby   Yes/No/Don't Know
by drinking breast milk   Yes/No/Don't Know
by sneezing and coughing   Yes/No/Don't Know
by vaginal intercourse   Yes/No/Don't Know

17 When having sex can:
a man catch the AIDS virus from an infected man?
                                  Yes/No/Don't Know
a man catch the AIDS virus from an infected woman?
                                  Yes/No/Don't Know
a woman catch the AIDS virus from an infected man?
                                  Yes/No/Don't Know
a woman catch the AIDS virus from an infected woman?
                                  Yes/No/Don't Know

18 Give the three groups of people you think are most at risk of catching the AIDS virus:
a) . . . .
b) . . . .
c) . . . .

19 Which of the following kills off the AIDS virus outside the body?
heat   Yes/No/Don't Know
soap and water   Yes/No/Don't Know
disinfectants   Yes/No/Don't Know

20 If you have sex using a condom, does it protect you against getting AIDS?
                                  Yes/No/Don't Know

21 If you had a friend who was worried about AIDS, where do you think he/she should go first for help? (circle one only)
casualty department of local hospital
family doctor
family planning clinic
sexually transmitted disease clinic
school nurse
teacher
parents
AIDS telephone 'help' line
friends

22   Write the numbers 1 to 4 against the things which worry you
most—in the order that you find them most worrying (1
against the most worrying, 2 against the next most worrying,
and so on)—among the following:
failing your exams
leaving home as a young man or woman
catching AIDS
a parent or brother or sister dying
being out of work
having an argument with your parents
being arrested for using drugs
not having a 'steady' friend of the opposite sex
your favourite pet dying

Thank you very much for answering this questionnaire

What a sweat filling this in—sure I got half the answers
wrong.

7th November

Think Charlie must have lost my phone number again. No way
I'm going to phone him.

8th November

AIDS again at school today. The teachers gave us the
answers—and there will be more answers tomorrow. They're
obsessed.

AIDS—All Your Questions Answered

(1) What does 'AIDS' stand for?
'Acquired Immune Deficiency Syndrome'. It was given this name
because the effect of the disease is to destroy the body's normal
defences (immune system) to infections.

(2) What causes AIDS?
A virus. Most AIDS infections are caused by a virus called HIV1.
Researchers have found another virus that causes AIDS called
HIV2, and others are being discovered.

(3) What does 'HIV' stand for?
'Human Immunodeficiency Virus' because it affects the body's immune system.

(4) When was AIDS first discovered?
It was first noticed in America in the early 1980s. However there was one case in America in the 1970s of a boy who died from a mysterious and previously unknown disease. They saved some of his blood, and when they tested it in the 1980s they discovered that he might have been infected with the AIDS virus.

(5) How and where did it start?
We don't know. There are many theories including one that it may have come from a person coming into contact with a certain kind of 'green' monkey in Africa. It is then said to have spread to America via one airline steward who had many sexual partners.

(6) How many people in the UK have been diagnosed with the AIDS disease?
By the end of 1994, the number of AIDS cases had reached 10,304.

(7) How many of these people have died from AIDS?
By the end of 1994, 7,019 people had died.

(8) Can the AIDS virus be tested for straightaway?
You need to have a blood test in order to tell whether or not you have been infected by the AIDS virus, but it can take at least four months after getting the infection for the test to become positive.

(9) Does infection with the AIDS virus last for ever?
Yes, probably. Once you've got the AIDS virus, it appears that you have it for the rest of your life.

(10) If you're infected with the AIDS virus, do you get ill immediately?
No. You may be infected with the virus and show no signs of illness for years, maybe in some cases—never. However, even if you are not ill, YOU WILL STILL BE INFECTIOUS TO OTHERS.

(11) Do all people infected with the AIDS virus die from it?
At the moment some people who are infected with the virus do not seem to develop the disease. However, year by year, of all the

people who have the virus infection, gradually more and more do develop the disease. Once someone has developed the disease, the chances of dying are high because at the moment there is no cure.

(12) **What are the symptoms**?
The first signs of being ill with the AIDS disease can be very vague and very much like other illnesses. Tiredness and swollen glands are common, but having these doesn't mean you've got AIDS. Other symptoms are loss of weight and repeated infections. Whether or not you are worried about having AIDS will depend upon what you have been doing and whether you have put yourself at risk of getting it.

(13) **Is there a cure**?
No. At present there is no cure, and no immediate likelihood of one. Drugs are being tried, which may slow the disease down. Scientists are also working on developing a vaccine to protect against AIDS, but when it is discovered it will take many years to test it.

(14) **Can the AIDS virus be passed on even if you don't know you have it**?
Yes. The blood test only becomes positive several months after the virus has got into the body. Not everyone infected with the virus knows that they've got it, because they won't have had a blood test.

(15) **Where will the virus be in someone who is infected**?
Definitely in: blood, semen, vaginal secretions. It can also be found in: saliva, faeces, tears and urine—but only in very small amounts and it is not thought that you can catch it from them. It is not found in the skin.

(16) **How can a person catch the AIDS virus**?
Definitely from an infected person by: sharing needles, anal intercourse, an infected mother to her unborn baby, vaginal intercourse. Some people in the past have caught AIDS by being given a blood transfusion with infected blood or infected blood products (including people being treated for haemophilia). But all blood and blood products in the UK are now tested, and people

who are at high risk of having AIDS are asked not to be blood donors.

You CANNOT catch it by: touching door knobs, sharing dishes and glasses, using lavatory seats, holding hands, having head lice, sneezing and coughing, and swimming in swimming pools.

So far, it is thought that you CANNOT catch it by: kissing or sharing toothbrushes.

(17) **When having sex:**
A man can catch the AIDS virus from an infected man or woman.
A woman can catch it from an infected man.
There are no known cases of a woman catching it from an infected woman.

(18) **Groups of people most at risk:**
The groups of people most at risk in Britain were homosexuals and bisexuals, intravenous drug users and prostitutes; and, previously, people having blood transfusions and haemophiliacs. But now, increasingly, it is also someone having sex with someone of the opposite sex without using a condom. Similarly, in certain parts of Africa it is much more a disease of both sexes; and everyone changing sexual partners frequently is at risk. IF YOU AND YOUR PARTNER ONLY HAVE SEX WITH ONE ANOTHER THEN YOU WON'T GET AIDS (unless you are silly enough to use intravenous drugs).

(19) **What kills the AIDS virus?**
The AIDS virus is very sensitive, and outside the body it doesn't survive very well. It is also killed off by heat, soap and water, and disinfectants. This is why you cannot catch AIDS from an infected person from cups, door knobs and lavatory seats.

(20) **Do condoms protect you from catching AIDS?**
Yes—almost completely. It is a very good idea to use them always. REMEMBER THEY ALSO PROTECT YOU FROM OTHER SEXUALLY TRANSMITTED DISEASES AND FROM PREGNANCY.

(21) **Who can you go to for help?**
If you're worried, you ought to talk to someone about your fears. It doesn't really matter who, as long as you find them sympathetic. If you have reason to be really worried, the only way to find out if you are or are not infected with the virus is to have a blood test, and for that you need to see a doctor.

(22) What worries you most?
The survey of your class showed that the top four worries were:
(1) being out of work
(2) a parent or brother or sister dying
(3) failing your exams
(4) not having a 'steady' friend of the opposite sex.
Not surprisingly, this is very different for different people at
different times. There is no right or wrong thing to worry about!

Mark (rated by me as only 2/10) seemed to know all the
answers. Not surprising, seeing what he gets up to. I'd have to
be really desperate to say 'yes' to him!

Don't think Mum will ever speak to Sal again. We had this
discussion about AIDS. I asked Sal about her boyfriends in
the last year, and Sal counted on the fingers of both hands—
just to wind Mum up. Mum went spare. To calm her down, I
asked how many boyfriends she'd had before she met Dad. No
answer.

Just thinking about Mum and Dad doing it turns me off. I
wonder what they actually got up to before they were married.
You'd think they were both totally innocent the way they tell
it, but I just don't believe it. Certainly not judging from Mum's
old photos Pete found in a box at Aunty Pam's!

9th November
CHARLIE PHONED! He really meant it about not phoning me
because he didn't have my number. I'm seeing him next week.

Financial

Aids

18

21st November

Still missing Pete—much to my surprise. Even the teasing.

My money situation is crucial. I don't think I get enough pocket-money, so I did a quick survey among my friends. Poor Kate only gets £2.50—don't know how she manages, but of course she doesn't buy sweets or anything. Mary gets the most. Her parents are divorced too, and she gets £15 a week from her mum AND £15 from her dad. She says she bids them against one another and makes the other one feel guilty. Most of us seem to get around £7, which is what I'm meant to get—when Mum remembers. I used to get this as an allowance of £30 a month, but would blow it all the first day on a pair of shoes. Mum says it's only for the cinema, presents, CDs, bus fares, make-up and magazines. She buys the clothes and shoes.

Seeing that we work at school, I think we ought to get paid for going there. Then I'd be independent of having to ask Mum all the time. Charlie's working as a garage mechanic apprentice and making £120 a week. Sounded like a fortune till he pointed out that some goes on tax, he pays his mum and dad £30 a week for food and lodging, he has to pay for all his own travel to get to the garage, all his own clothes, AND for taking me to the cinema! I said I'd pay for myself the first time, and then found I couldn't as I didn't have any money. I'm glad he insisted on paying.

I used to be richer when I did baby-sitting, but I've been put off by my experiences. I suppose I could start again, seeing I'm so broke. Or I could get a job like Mary. She works as a glass collector in a wine bar on Saturday and Sunday nights. She gets £7 for two and a half hours. John used to work in the local hamburger joint and got £15 for six hours. Now he works in a café bar which he hates. He gets £18 for nine hours' work. It's really slave labour and it tires him out.

22nd November

A letter from Pete! Maybe he misses ME!

Dear Susie,
Well, here I am, a real university student at last. I thought it would be a doddle. But after you left, panic set in. Will anyone like me? What if no one talks to me? Will they all be cleverer than me? I'm going to drop out. I want a year off.
Mum was great when I rang up. You know how understanding she can be when she wants. 'You'll be fine, everyone is in the same boat. Just be yourself.' The soundest piece of advice—that.
There was some mail waiting for me. (Goodness I'm popular, I thought as I filled a carrier bag with a thousand bits of paper.) The letters all turned out to be about me paying money to join some society or other.

My room. Mmmmmh, not bad—small. But I thought a few posters would probably do the trick. I didn't unpack, but went out to find some people to meet. I wasn't going to spend the next five years on my tod. Didn't know a soul. Be American, I kept telling myself. Impose yourself. 'Hi, I'm Pete, how's it going?' 'Have a nice day.' Suddenly it didn't seem so easy, but I've made some friends and I'll tell you all about them when I see you at Christmas.
I'm missing you all, and my room, and you'd better all write to me. Could you get Mum to send me all the latest football clippings from the back of the local rag? Could you send me my blue pullover from the top drawer in my room (it might need a bit of a wash first), also my other pair of shoes, my folder with the lined paper, and my second pen. And Susie, you have my 'Don't Sit on the Grass— Smoke it' T-shirt. I know I gave it to you but now I want it back. Also my medical dictionary, and my book on 'medical geniuses'. If all this is too much trouble, you could give them all to Sandy who's coming up to see me next week—I hope.
love from your brother

Health Freak Pete

P.S. Sharing a kitchen with a bloke who's managed to create an ideology to defend the fact that he's a lazy bastard. He never cleans up after himself. I'm going to use this excuse when I get back home. P.P.S. Forgot to post this letter when I wrote it five weeks ago! Sorry to hear Bov ate Pinko. I was hoping to experiment on Pinko when I came back at Christmas. You really should have been more careful. (He's a laugh a minute, my brother.)

Pete doesn't know about Charlie yet. Not sure I do really. I had a great time at the cinema last night. No attempted rape!

26th November

AIDS, AIDS, AIDS. Can't see why they call it AIDS when it doesn't aid anyone. Mary says Mini Willie's attitude is, 'I'll have to cut down on the girlies, and if I do have to jump into bed for a bonk then I'll use a johnny, 'cos I can't do without it altogether.'

I don't know one person with AIDS—but had to spend another whole afternoon talking about it and relationships at school today. Quite revealing about some of my friends. John said, 'If I caught it, I would try to make the rest of my life more exciting and just as I wanted it. I wouldn't sleep with anybody else so that no one would catch it from me. I don't think I'd tell anyone. I'd probably lose a lot of friends as they'd think I was dirty. I would probably just tell my parents and the person I caught it from, so that they wouldn't give it to anyone else. I think I'd go to a place where other people had AIDS, so I wouldn't feel odd.'

Mary was really awful and said if she caught AIDS, she'd try to give it to as many people as possible and try to take them with her. She said she'd then be so bitter and angry and upset that she'd probably kill herself before kicking the bucket.

While we were talking, a scribbled note was passed from Kate who sits in front of me, saying,

> 'AIDS advice—don't be silly
> Put a condom on his willie.'

As I was laughing, Mr Rogers (remember the bad breath?) found me with it. He read it, went bright red, and then collapsed trying not to laugh too. He had been explaining that the chances of a man without the AIDS virus catching it from a woman with the virus, during one-off sexual intercourse, was about 1 in 1,000, and the other way round (we women always have it worse) was 1 in 100. But most people don't just have sex once!

Emma thought that AIDS had changed her outlook on sex, and though it wouldn't scare her away from having sex, it would make her more cautious. She'd be sure to know the person she was having sex with, and would want to ask her partner about his previous sex life. She was worried though that he might think it rude and offensive. Mr Rogers said she shouldn't be afraid to ask what other sexual partners someone had had. It might make all the difference between life and death. And it wasn't just because of AIDS, but because of all the other sexually transmitted diseases you could get as well, like chlamydia which really scares me.

I wish the scientists would find a cure for AIDS, because I'm frightened of catching it when I'm older. People joke about it, but don't really think about what would happen if they caught it. I think it's becoming a serious problem in the world, and it's frightening to think that if you go with someone, you don't know whether they have got it or not. If I found out that I had AIDS, and there was an experiment to help find a cure, I'd be willing to help.

I don't like to see babies on television who have been born with AIDS. They don't even know that they have it, but they are going to die. Watching TV programmes about AIDS is really depressing, because the amount of people who are catching AIDS is going up. What I particularly didn't like was the programme about a man who was so angry that he was going to die from AIDS that he went with everybody he could, so as to spread the disease. I think that's really selfish—like what Mary said. I also watched this play about a man who caught AIDS. He had to tell his wife how he'd caught it, by going with another man. He got worse and worse. I think this programme must have got across to a lot of people, if they didn't forget it after a couple of weeks.

'Thought for the Day' written on a toilet wall at school: 'Last one to get AIDS is a wanker'.

29th November

I think it's going well with Charlie—at least I hope so. I hardly dare write about it or tell anybody about him, in case it all goes wrong. Sometimes I worry about whether he does fancy me—he's so unpushy. Today I found a four-leaf clover, so everything is bound to be all right.

3rd December

Don't know how Pete manages it—wanting to be a doctor. I think I'd be hopeless. I needed Pete's expertise this morning but it was Sita who knew what to do.

We were all outside, between lessons, me avoiding the usual crowd over in one corner smoking fags, when suddenly this boy from year 9 fell to the ground and started jerking around. I think everyone thought he was joking to begin with, but then a crowd gathered round and just stared. No one knew what to do and we were all getting scared, thinking he was dying or something, when Sita pushed past me and told everyone to stand back and not to touch him and that he'd be all right. I was really impressed.

The boy stopped jerking after what seemed ages, but was probably only a minute. Then he seemed to go to sleep. Sita pushed him on to his side, and said this was so that he wouldn't breathe in his sick if he threw up. She said you should do that if someone was unconscious for any reason.

Mr Rogers arrived at this point and sent everyone back into their classrooms—Sita too, which seemed a bit unfair as she had done everything properly. Afterwards Sita said she had a cousin who used to have fits when he was little, but it only happened when he got a high temperature. Mr Rogers came and said 'thank you' to her later, and explained that the boy had had epilepsy for some time. Normally he didn't have any problems, as long as he took his tablets every morning, but he had obviously forgotten for the last few days.

I think Mr Rogers knew we were all scared because he reassured us that epilepsy affects about 5 people in every 1,000. With medicines, most people with epilepsy can live perfectly normal lives today, as long as people let them. The worst problem that epileptics have to put up with is other people being frightened of them and treating them as if they are ill all the time, or mental or something. They can do everything everybody else does. They can do jobs, play sports, even swim (as long as they are with somebody).

But it was scary, and I can see how people think epileptics might die when they are having an attack. Mr Rogers said that that was very rare. He said if you see someone having an attack, all you have to do is make sure they can't hurt

themselves against anything while they are jerking about. He said that people used to think they should put something into epileptics' mouths to stop them biting their tongue. This is now thought to be wrong, because they might choke on it, or they might bite you by mistake. If you leave them alone, the attack will stop after a few minutes. Then you should do what Sita had done, and lay them on their side, till they wake up. Normally they didn't have to go to hospital or anything, and Sita and I even saw the boy back in the playground in the afternoon.

I think he should have said something to Sita, but maybe he didn't know it was her who had helped him, or maybe he was embarrassed. Pete's home next week, so I'll be able to tell him about it.

19

An *Itchy* and *Freaky* **Christmas**

10th December

Pete's home. His usual arrogant little self, and a worse 'know all' now he's at university. I think he's still hot on Sandy, though I'm not so sure the reverse is true. Didn't tell him I saw her snogging James. I do mind for him but I don't want to be the person to have to tell him.

I told him all about having to cope with an epileptic fit in school. Nice to be able to tell HIM something for a change.

17th December

Pete's birthday. He's 18! He's not having a party as he had one in Nottingham—with a friend who's also 18 this week. Mum asked if he'd like another one at home, but I think she was rather relieved when he said he'd rather we all went out for a meal.

18th December

Charlie's been away on a training course for two weeks. Now he's back, we're seeing quite a lot of one another. Mum won't let me see him during the week in term time as she thinks it interferes with my work. Mary's mum lets her go out all the time. I sometimes think she doesn't really care about Mary. Although I get angry with Mum, and argue with her about this, actually it's quite good. I can get on with my work and tell Charlie it's all Mum's fault!

All that stuff Pete said about 'sexual sequencing' seems to be true, though I hadn't really considered it before. I thought it was something that only happened to other people, or in books. It certainly never occurred to me during the heat of the action!

I know that Charlie fancies me because he's always looking at me out of the corner of his eye. His hand sometimes brushes against mine as if by accident. He smiles at me a lot, and sits close to me when there are other seats around. He looks at other parts of my body, and he's always nervously checking to see how I respond to what he is saying. Sometimes he even agrees with what I say when I know he really doesn't. I thought only girls did this! He always seems to be licking his lips, which makes me wonder what his expectations are! He has kissed me, but I don't think he's got much experience.

He seemed a bit cool when we first went out. Perhaps my pheromones weren't right, but I haven't had a fag in ages, as Charlie did say something about not liking girls who smell like ashtrays. I was wrong about him being into drugs—he's like Pete about that kind of thing. I'm not sure we have a lot in common, but I like him.

It must be a nice job researching this 'sexual sequencing' stuff. Better than being a hairdresser, like Sally was (though perhaps that's all to do with sex as well). Sal thinks this science stuff is a load of rubbish and spoils it all anyway.

20th December

Pete's a problem at the moment. Things are not good between him and Sandy. He thinks she's two-timing him, which she is. He can't understand what girls are about. Long list of complaints: 'Why can't she say what she wants?' 'Why does she have to keep crying and hinting there's some terrible dark secret?' 'Why did she keep saying she'd tell him about it and then didn't?' He thinks she's trying to tantalize him. Then after being mean to him, she started flirting with him in the pub. She became really angry when Pete rejected her and said she was just doing it because she was drunk. Pete doesn't deserve to be treated like this.

Showed Pete the AIDS questionnaire. He got half the questions wrong, but said it didn't matter as he wasn't in the high risk group. I sometimes wonder. Anyway, I told him it *did* matter, as not only people in the high risk group get AIDS.

Pete has learnt something at medical school about sexually transmitted diseases, though he's not sure how useful some of it would be today. Apparently they used to treat syphilis by applying a roast turnip 'as hot as the patient can bear' to the affected part. I asked, 'What part's that?'

He said that nowadays, if you stick to just one person, then there is virtually no risk of catching AIDS. Five partners a year and you could be spreading to 3,905 people in interrelated contacts over five years. Twenty partners and you're up to three million. Way beyond my maths but obviously not beyond Pete's.

23rd December

Pete's worrying about his health. I think it's all to do with Sandy's dad having died from a heart attack. He was only 56 but smoked twenty a day and 'liked' his food. Pete wants to have the amount of cholesterol in his blood measured. He's sure it must be high. He's heard that most heart attacks are caused by having too much cholesterol in your blood. Apparently almost everybody (70 %) has a high cholesterol level in this country compared with America, which is why they think we have more heart attacks than anywhere else in the world.

What have they done right in America that we're not doing here? Shouldn't have asked, should I? Not if I didn't want this half-hour lecture from Pete.

'*In America they eat wholemeal bread, wholemeal pasta, beans, baked potatoes in their jackets, lentils, brown rice . . .*'

I begged to go to the lav, it was the talk of all this fibre, but the avalanche had begun and wasn't to be diverted. My avalanche would just have to wait.

'*. . . take more regular exercise, drink skimmed milk rather than the full fat stuff, use low fat yoghurt instead of cream, use sunflower spreads instead of butter, cook in polyunsaturated vegetable oil and drain it off the food afterwards, eat more fish, the white bits of the chicken (not the skin), and less red meat . . .*'

Please, please, please I'm bursting!

'*. . . grilled rather than fried food, no chips or sausages, no salt added at the table. We can make do with one-tenth of the salt we eat at the moment.*'

How did he know all these things? He's like a flipping encyclopaedia.

'*It's really up to us. If we buy these things, then the manufacturers will sell them. While we want chips, they'll sell chips. If the National Health Service is meant to be doing all this preventative stuff, then why isn't the government helping by at least making sure that all school meals are healthy. They must be thinking about it—they've started feeding baked beans to pigs as an experiment to reduce their cholesterol.*'

Just made it to the lav. When I got back, I told him about my success at school with the food questionnaire. Think he was nearly impressed but, as always, came back with more facts. How does he remember them all? Apparently teenage boys need about 2,500 calories per day, and teenage girls about 2,000 (and less than 30% of these calories should come from fat). And if they take lots of exercise, they need more.

Poor Pete, he's got a letter from Sandy and it's all off. Must be why Bov chose today to eat the two goldfish—Leroy and Marvin—that Sandy had given him. Better this way than it just Petering out, ha, ha.

Still off fags.

24th December
Daisy, Paul, and Aunty Jo came for a Christmas tea. They're staying with Aunty Pam so we'll see them again tomorrow. Aunty Jo's getting a divorce. Uncle Geoff's back from a spell in Bosnia and off with his floozie. Pity he didn't get blown up— the way he's treated Aunty Jo.

25th December
What a Christmas present. Woke up with an itchy bum. Must be worms again. Surely I'm too old for worms. Bet it's from my cousins. I catch everything from them.

Dad says you can't get worms that quickly. He really is the resident expert on all the nasty things we get. Says human worms come in almost as many varieties as Haagen Daas ice-cream. Long ones, short ones, thin ones, fat ones, flat ones, hermaphrodite ones. There are worms that travel round your body and lay eggs in mentionable and unmentionable places, ones that make you thin, ones that make your bum itch, ones that are caught from animals, ones that are caught from eating uncooked food, ones that are caught from other human beings—on and on. The commonest one is the thread worm (also known as the pin worm, one of the nematodes or *Enterobius vermicularis*—but most commonly referred to as just 'the worms') which Dad said was the one I had.

He talks about them as if they were almost friendly! 'They're innocuous little things that inhabit the gut of about one in three of us, most of the time. They come in two sexes—the 'hers' are bigger than the 'hims'—13mm compared with 5mm—and with a diameter of 0.5mm compared with 0.2mm. The poor old pregnant worm is really just made up of two huge wombs—ready to spill out—while all the male has for himself is a curly tail! They mainly live in your gut, near your appendix, and the female creeps out at night to lay her eggs on the skin around your bottom, which is why yours is itching.'

Dad said I'd got worms from someone who'd scratched their own bum because it was itchy. They'd got the eggs under their fingernails, and then touched some food which I'd eaten, so it had all got spread around. Yugh. Don't like the idea that I've eaten something from somebody else's bum. Now they're squirming around inside me having a Christmas feast.

Dad says they are easy to get rid of. All I have to do is get some anti-worm medicine, but I can't go to the chemist because they're all closed. The whole family will have to take the medicine—like the anti-louse stuff. It gives your insides a thorough clear-out and gets rid of the worms. But for the next two days, I'm going to have to put up with an itchy bum.

Pete says he's got them too. He wanted to use this as an excuse not to go to Aunty Pam's for lunch. No way Mum was going to let us off though. She said it was up to us, BUT . . . so we had to go. As if going there wasn't bad enough—we even had a lecture from Mum in the car about manners and being nice to Daisy and Paul.

Aunty Pam and Uncle Bob's house was reeking of resident dog shit and cat pee, as usual. I sometimes wonder whether it's always the same turd and piddle that they've never cleared up.

There was a four-hour interval before the meal was served up. All jolly Christmas spirit had sunk to zero. What with Uncle Bob being plastered, Gran snoring, Dad with nothing left to say, Mum trying to fill in the ten-minute conversational gaps, Aunty Jo sobbing quietly, Aunty Pam in the kitchen swearing, Daisy reading Aunty Pam's old knitting patterns, Pete and Paul completely disappeared—I just sat and scratched my bum.

I think Sal was right to go to her boyfriend's parents for Christmas. Wish I could have gone with her.

When the meal was finally served, no one could find Pete and Paul. I said they were probably upstairs smoking cannabis and getting high together. Daisy rushed upstairs (I think she wanted to try some too) but found only Dad, smoking a fag.

We finally found the boys in the garden playing football. They came in covered with mud and trod more dog shit into the new carpet. Paul tripped over the electric wire to the Christmas tree lights, and the tree fell on to the table. The result was 'needle soup'. Don't think it made it any worse. Aunty Pam definitely wins the Decrepit Aunt's 'Worst Cook of the Year' prize. I'm glad I'm a vegetarian. Uncle Bob's carving was worse than seeing the *Chain-Saw Gang Massacre* on video last week, and Aunty Pam had left the plastic bag of innards inside the turkey.

We had the wettest crackers I've ever known. Not one banger worked. Only Aunty Pam and Uncle Bob would wear their paper hats. Everyone else complained that they were too small. I wonder whether they find special morons to write the cracker jokes?

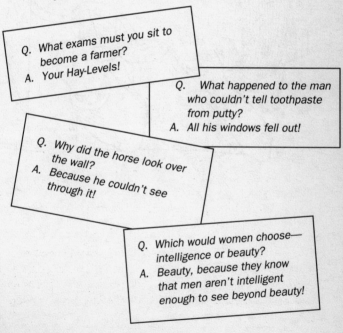

Q. What exams must you sit to become a farmer?
A. Your Hay-Levels!

Q. What happened to the man who couldn't tell toothpaste from putty?
A. All his windows fell out!

Q. Why did the horse look over the wall?
A. Because he couldn't see through it!

Q. Which would women choose—intelligence or beauty?
A. Beauty, because they know that men aren't intelligent enough to see beyond beauty!

Pete frisked the plum pudding for money, but Aunty Pam's far too mean for that. There was no brandy left to light it, because Uncle Bob had drunk it all. He was so slewed, he even forgot to ask if I'd got a boyfriend yet. The only time I had wanted him to ask, too. Just so I could say, 'Yes' at last!

Index

Index

Index

305143299-